Gardening for Birdwatchers

By Mike Toms, Ian Wilson & Barley Wilson

This book is dedicated to the late Dilys Breese

Published by the
British Trust for Ornithology

British Trust for Ornithology
The Nunnery
Thetford
Norfolk
IP24 2PU
01842-750050
gbw@bto.org
www.bto.org

First published in 2008

British Trust for Ornithology

ISBN 978-1-906204-30-3

Text: Mike Toms, Ian Wilson, Barley Wilson
Design & Layout: Mike Toms (BTO)
Printed by: Reflex Litho, St. Helen's Way, Thetford, Norfolk, IP24 1HG

Front cover: Willow Warbler by Jill Pakenham

ENVIRONMENT
This book, including its cover, is printed on Greencoat Plus Velvet – a paper which contains 80% recycled post-consumer fibre.

Contents

This book would not have been possible without the support of the BTO/CJ Garden BirdWatch Steering Group (especially Pam Rhodes, Chris Whittles and the late Dilys Breese), Graham Appleton, Margaret Askew, Nigel Clark, Emily Coleman, Helen Kramer, Theresa Mason, Jacky Prior, Heather Pymar, Sandra Sparkes and Paul Stancliffe. As ever, the generosity of those photographers providing images for the BTO image library has ensured the inclusion of stunning images without which the book would have been pale by comparison. Special thanks are due to Dawn Balmer, Andrew Cleave, CJ WildBird Foods Ltd., Dave Goulson, John Harding, Graham Jarvis, William Logan, Christine M Matthews, Jill Pakenham and Paul Sterry. The creation of the BTO Nunnery Garden was only made possible through the support and generosity of CJ WildBird Foods Ltd., Emorsgate Wild Seeds, Gardman Ltd., Norfolk Museums and Heritage Partnership, Northumbrian Water, Pam Rhodes, Pearsons, WREN and the hard work of Natural Gardens, ably assisted by BTO staff (especially Theresa Mason and Chris Nichols).

Section Headers: John Harding (Page 7 – Fieldfare, Page 61 – Robin, Page 77 – Starling, Page 89 – Chaffinch), Mike Toms (Page 15 – Nunnery pond, Page 29 – RHS Chelsea).

Two hundred years ago an eccentric Yorkshireman called Charles Waterton set out to turn his patch, all 260 acres of it, into a paradise for birds. He had a lot of good ideas and some decidedly perverse ones. He built a high wall round the entire property to exclude dogs and casual disturbance. Foxes were trapped and deported, and even badgers were shown the door, in rather drastic moves to reduce the hazards to birds. He banned shooting altogether, threatening to strangle his keeper if he shot any Barn Owls, and forbade boating on his lake during the waterfowl breeding season. He experimented with various nestboxes designed to encourage owls (and Starlings!) and Sand Martins to breed. He ensured, too, the luxurious growth of Ivy, correctly deciding that it was a wholly beneficial plant which would provide food and shelter for birds without damaging his trees.

One way or another, Squire Waterton was far in advance of his contemporaries in understanding the general principles of wildlife management on an ecological basis, in spite of his aberrations. He successfully sued the owners of a nearby soap works when he considered their effluent was polluting his lake but the law, reflecting the spirit of an age when industry was of key importance, awarded him derisory damages. Waterton's relations with fellow workers in his field were inclined to be fairly hot-tempered. He cordially despised the museum workers, calling them 'closet naturalists' (this was at a time when taxonomy, the science of classification, was seen as the only fit pursuit for a professional), and positively gloried in field-work, as well as in his amateur status. I like to think he would have been a founding member of the British Trust for Ornithology, the organisation which has done most to link the enthusiast with the scientist in celebrating back-garden nature reserves.

A garden is a splendid thing but it is the birds which decorate it as much as the flower borders. Both are colourful, both mark the coming and going of the seasons, but birds offer the added value of song and dance. We all have mixed reasons for attracting and feeding birds in our gardens. It is good to think that we're contributing to conservation but many of us simply like to see birds up front and close. And why not? Nothing enlivens a dull, winter garden more than the thin song of a Robin or a constant flurry of birds around the feeders.

So keep up the good work; grow bird-friendly plants, share your crusts as well as peanuts and cunning seed-mixes. Garden bird reserves contribute mightily to a healthy environment. Even while we wash the dishes in the kitchen, we can check the numbers of Goldfinches attracted to thistle heads. Bird gardening is a pleasure, but bird-garden science measures the health of the nation's wildlife. The symbiotic relationship between amateur birders and professional ornithologists, not typical of the academic world, is something to be cherished. Counting birds is more fun than it sounds and submitting records to the BTO/CJ Garden BirdWatch is doing your bit for the planet.

Tony Soper
South Devon, April 2008

The BTO Nunnery Gardens were established both to enhance the wildlife value of the grounds around the British Trust for Ornithology's (BTO's) Norfolk headquarters and to provide a working framework for articles and advice for those interested in wildlife-friendly gardening. From the outset it was clear that Natural Gardens, the garden design company selected for this task, had very similar ideas to BTO staff over what was wanted and how it could best be achieved. The end result is a series of gardens which reflects the range of growing conditions seen in different gardens across the country, while, at the same time, producing something that is totally in keeping with the surroundings of the Nunnery and its unique history.

From the traditional garden, showcasing how new elements can be readily incorporated into an existing garden setting, through to the wildflower meadow, there is plenty of inspiration here for those gardeners wishing to increase the value of their own gardens for birds and other wildlife. This book uses the backdrop of the BTO Nunnery Gardens to illustrate various wildlife-friendly gardening techniques, drawing upon the scientific literature to support (or refute) perceived wisdom about how wildlife gardening should be practised and to suggest plants, planting schemes and other features that can be used to attract birds and other garden wildlife.

The first section of this book tackles the question of how birds use gardens, identifying those features that are attractive to birds and highlighting how this knowledge can help you improve the attractiveness of your own garden. The second section looks at some of the guiding principles behind wildlife-friendly gardening, tackling the thorny issue of native versus alien plants and their respective value for wildlife, before looking at some of the basic gardening techniques essential for developing a wildlife-friendly garden. The remaining sections of the book (its core sections) explore the different elements that can be incorporated into your own garden. Some, like the sections on bird feeding and the selection of fruiting shrubs, are targeted directly at birds; others are targeted at those insects which will, in turn, attract and support insectivorous birds.

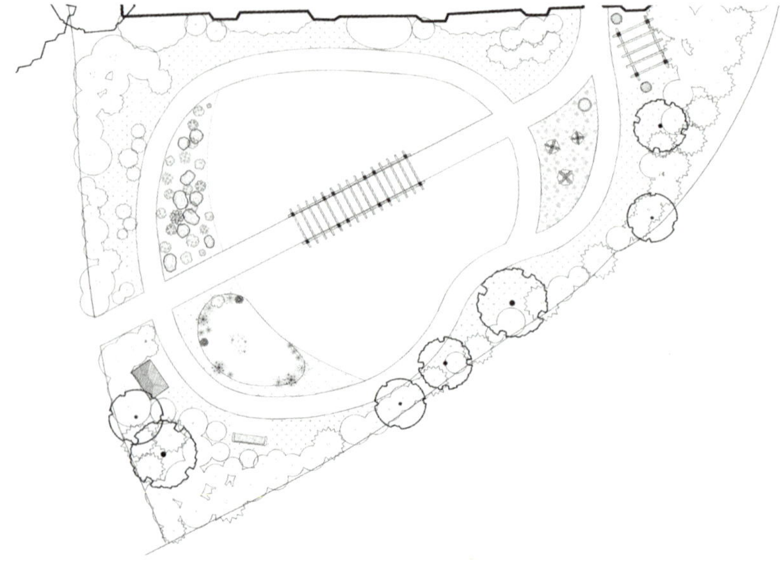

BIRDS AND GARDENS

A nation of gardeners

Joseph Addison, the English essayist and Whig politician, once remarked that he valued his garden more for being full of Blackbirds than of cherries and *'very frankly gave them* [the Blackbirds] *fruit for their songs'*. These sentiments find resonance in many of us; a 'nation of gardeners' gleaning enjoyment from most, though not necessarily all, of the wildlife that a garden supports.

There are many different forms of wildlife within an average garden, much of which goes unnoticed, but it would be fair to say that the greatest pleasure seems to be derived from the birds that are present. After all, they are one of the most visible components of the garden fauna, being attractively marked, largely diurnal and full of character. As such, they add a quality to our lives, reinforcing associations with the wider natural world.

The extent to which an individual sets out to manage their garden for birds is debatable; it is clear that a garden serves many different purposes and its value to birds or other wildlife is often a secondary consequence of management targeted towards other goals. The nature of our gardens, their value to wildlife and the management practices employed within them have changed over time. They also vary according to culture, class, background, fashion and personal taste.

Introduced to Britain by the Romans, the first recognisable gardens would have had ornamental as well as functional properties, a theme that slowly developed over time through the middle ages and beyond to the present day. By the time of the Tudors, the expanding horizons made possible through exploration brought new plants to our shores, leading to further developments in garden structure and form. The 16th and 17th centuries saw kitchen gardens prosper – that element of functionality still central to the role of the garden within society, or at least that component of society financially able to maintain such a garden. During the 19th Century, however, a mass of plant introductions revolutionised the role of gardens. Texts by William Robinson (cited by many authors as the father of the English flower garden) and Gertrude Jekyll (with her soft, herbaceous plantings) set the scene for the development of what we recognise today as a typical garden.

In recent years, the nature of the modern garden has shifted further away from the functional; a decrease in average

Young male Blackbird – John Harding

garden size, coupled with increasingly busy lives, has meant that gardens have become 'outdoor rooms' used for leisure and relaxation, rather than for the cultivation of fruit and vegetables. Viewed within this context it is apparent that the garden (within a modern, western European society) provides an environment within which an individual can *engage, confront and understand the changing natural world.*' (Bhatti & Church 2001). However, it is important to remember that a garden is not a natural habitat, it is nature under control – even if the degree of control varies from one garden to another.

The notion that the British are a nation of gardeners has good supporting evidence. As Stefan Buczacki notes in his book 'Garden Natural History', there is *'greater depth and breadth of fine public and private gardens in Britain today than anywhere else.'* He attributes this to our tradition of being owner-occupiers of domestic properties with land attached. The most recently published statistics support this claim by demonstrating that some 70% of us are owner-occupiers. Not everyone will have land attached to their property but most do, or have access to shared space.

What we do with the space afforded by having a garden is up to us and so is the extent to which we adopt management practices that benefit wildlife. A recent report, published by the Horticultural Trades Association and based on a 2007 poll, found a clear link between the act of gardening and concern for the environment, demonstrating that gardeners were more concerned about a wider range of environmental issues than non-gardeners. This reinforces our belief that gardeners have a role to play in encouraging wildlife and that they will be willing participants in the process of increasing the wildlife value of the garden environment.

Welcoming wildlife

There has been increasing interest in the role of private gardens as nature reserves. They occupy some 10% of the available land area within the United Kingdom and this makes them (when viewed as a whole) an important habitat at the national level. Typically, however, these gardens do not exist as a single continuous entity but are, instead, present as a highly fragmented resource, often embedded within other habitats that have little or no wildlife value. Despite this, there is plenty of scientific evidence to support the assertion that gardens are of value to wildlife. Importantly, private gardens make a significant contribution to the amount of urban green space and remain the main contributor to urban biodiversity (Cannon 1999).

The isolation of many gardens from 'natural' habitats within the wider countryside is likely to be less of a problem for mobile species, like birds, which are perfectly able to reach and utilise gardens and the resources that they contain. Habitat-specific density estimates, derived from the BTO/JNCC/RSPB Breeding Bird Survey (BBS) suggest that 62% of the House Sparrow population, 54% of the Starling population and 33% of the Blackbird population breeds within human-occupied sites (Newson *et al.* 2005). Such figures highlight the value of gardens and other urbanised habitats for breeding birds.

The BTO/CJ Garden BirdWatch scheme has shown gardens to be important for birds at other times of the year. Many bird species show a peak in their use of gardens during the winter, a time of the year when food may be difficult to find within other habitats. Farmland species (such as Yellowhammer, Reed Bunting and Tree Sparrow) tend to visit rural gardens late in the winter, at just the time when seed availability within farmland is likely to be at its lowest.

Other organisms also utilise gardens, with the adaptable 'habitat generalists' more likely to use gardens than those creatures with a greater degree of specialisation in their habitat requirements (known as 'habitat specialists'). For species that are less mobile, gardens are only likely to be used where they are close to, or within, the 'natural' habitats used by the species. Nevertheless, individual gardens can support a wide range of other wildlife, including many species that are rare or threatened at the national level. This makes welcoming wildlife into your garden all the more worthwhile.

Estate housing – Mike Toms

Changes taking place within the wider countryside, in particular the management practices employed on farmland and the continued pressures placed on land by urbanisation, are likely to further increase the value of gardens for wildlife. However, this is dependent upon the nature of any new gardens that are created and the social attitudes towards their management once they have been established. For example, the trend for high-density housing, that has been stimulated by both Government policy and the dominance of the private sector in home construction, is likely to result in gardens that are less suitable for wildlife than the sorts of gardens established a generation ago. Enhancing the wildlife value of these new housing schemes requires inputs at the planning stage, viewing planned gardens not in isolation but within the wider context of the development as a whole. Although this landscape level approach is beyond the scope of this book, it is something which is likely to receive increasing attention over the coming years.

Why birds use gardens

Most gardens are likely to provide a number of different resources for a bird, including opportunities for nesting, roosting and feeding. Not all gardens will provide all of these resources and not all bird species will view the resources in the same way, so it is important to understand how and why birds use gardens. Such an understanding can help when determining what you need to do to make your garden more attractive to visiting birds (Toms 2007).

Observations collected by participants in the BTO/CJ Garden BirdWatch have been used to examine the ways in which birds respond to different features within and around gardens (Chamberlain *et al.* 2004). The results of this work suggest that it is the surrounding habitats that are of the greatest importance in determining the occurrence of a species within a garden. Certain species of bird are most likely to be associated with rural gardens, others with those on the suburban fringe and a smaller number with urban properties (see box on opposite page).

However, garden size also has a strong influence, with larger gardens typically supporting a greater number of species than smaller ones. Interestingly, the BTO study found that Collared Dove, House Sparrow and Starling were most likely to occur in small gardens, perhaps reflecting the urban preferences of these species. Structural characters within the garden were also important for a number of species; these were typically

Birds and their use of different types of garden

The chances of a bird using your garden depends, in part, on whether your garden is urban (U), suburban (S) or rural (R). This table shows the sorts of gardens used by different birds, with solid circles representing the greatest degree of use, shaded circles the medium degree of use and open circles denoting the least used.

Species	U	S	R	Species	U	S	R
Sparrowhawk	○	◐	●	Nuthatch	○	●	◐
Feral Pigeon	●	◐	○	Treecreeper	○	●	◐
Woodpigeon	○	◐	●	Jay	○	◐	●
Collared Dove	○	●	◐	Magpie	●	◐	○
Great Sp. Woodpecker	○	◐	●	Jackdaw	○	●	◐
Pied Wagtail	○	◐	●	Rook	○	◐	●
Wren	○	◐	●	Carrion Crow	○	◐	●
Dunnock	○	◐	●	Starling	●	◐	○
Robin	○	◐	●	House Sparrow	●	◐	○
Blackbird	○	◐	●	Tree Sparrow	○	◐	●
Song Thrush	○	●	◐	Chaffinch	○	◐	●
Mistle Thrush	○	◐	●	Brambling	○	◐	●
Blackcap	○	●	◐	Greenfinch	○	◐	●
Goldcrest	○	◐	●	Goldfinch	○	◐	●
Blue Tit	○	◐	●	Siskin	○	●	◐
Great Tit	○	◐	●	Bullfinch	○	◐	●
Coal Tit	○	◐	●	Reed Bunting	○	◐	●
Long-tailed Tit	○	◐	●	Yellowhammer	○	◐	●

those features that would provide cover for nesting or roosting. The provision of food was also found to be particularly important in determining the occurrence of individual species within gardens; the probability of occurrence for 24 species (of 41 studied) was significantly higher at sites where food was provided than it was at sites with no such provision.

So what does this all mean? Well, it means that the range of bird species using your garden will be determined, in the main, by where your garden is located. Two identical gardens, one in an urban location and the other in a rural location, will support a different number and range of bird species, with the rural garden doing rather better. The size of your garden also matters. The larger it is the more resources it is likely to contain (in terms of nesting and feeding opportunities) and the wider the range of bird species it is likely to support. Finally, the presence of nesting and feeding opportunities (a bird table, hanging feeders, fruiting bushes, *etc.*) will also have an influence. Increase these opportunities and you are likely to increase the attractiveness of your garden to birds (and other wildlife).

However, do not feel disheartened if you have a small courtyard garden in the middle of a large city. While you may never attract visiting Yellowhammers or

Reed Buntings, you are better placed than most to attract visiting (or nesting) House Sparrows or Starlings, both of which are red-listed as birds of conservation concern.

There is one final element to mention here and that is geography. There are more bird species breeding in the southeast of Britain than there are breeding in the northwest. Similarly, there are certain species that only occur in the southeast and others that only occur in the northwest. The location of your garden within Britain will have a direct influence on which species you have breeding locally and which, ultimately, you may have visiting your garden. Some gardens, such as those on the east coast of England or the Isles of Scilly, are best placed to receive scarce migrants during their period of migration. Not that all this really matters. It is what happens within your garden that is important and this book sets out to help you make the most of what you have got, increasing the pleasure that you derive from your garden and its visiting birds.

How birds use gardens

Most gardens are far too small to provide everything that a bird needs and so individual birds tend to range over a number of gardens, or beyond these into other habitats. Some species are very mobile outside of the breeding season and may visit different gardens many hundreds of miles apart over the course of a single winter. Others arrive in British gardens from breeding grounds elsewhere in Europe. For example, some of your wintering Blackbirds may have arrived from Poland, joining Greenfinches from Norway, Chaffinches from Sweden and Blackcaps from Germany.

Things are far more stable during the breeding season, with individual birds tied to their breeding territory and typically only ranging over a small area. Because of this, and because nesting opportunities within gardens are often lacking, a smaller range of species use gardens during the breeding season than are present in the winter. So, there is a clear seasonality to how birds use gardens and there is also a daily pattern of garden use. Both of these are strongly influenced by food availability and it is perhaps not that surprising that much of the activity is focused on bird tables and hanging bird feeders.

Take three birds...

Not all gardens are equal. As we have seen some species are more likely to turn up in an urban garden than a rural one. Such differences may also vary with season. As the following graphs show, House Sparrows prefer urban gardens, Robins rural gardens and Goldfinches vary their use of garden with season.

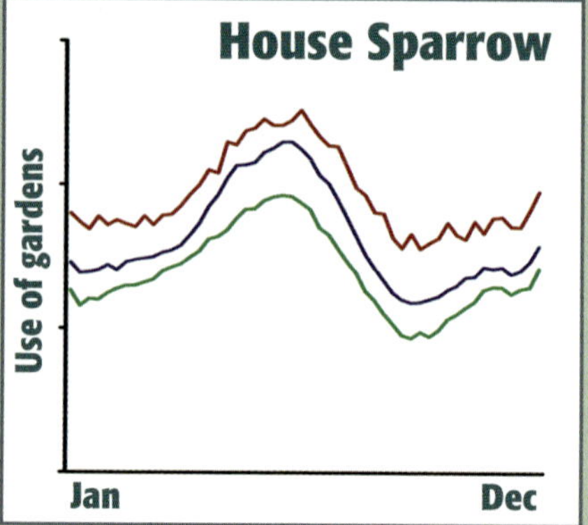

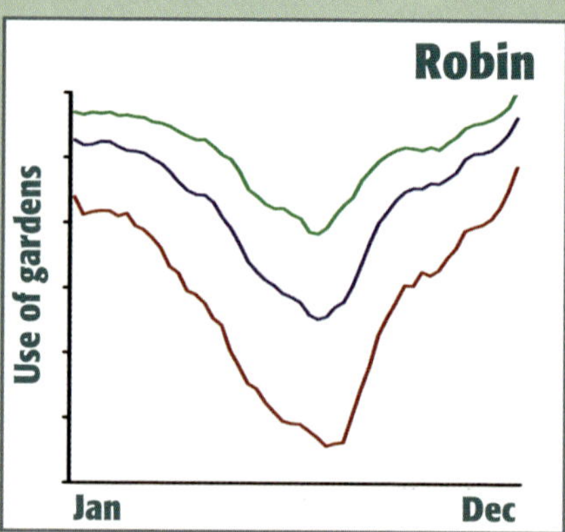

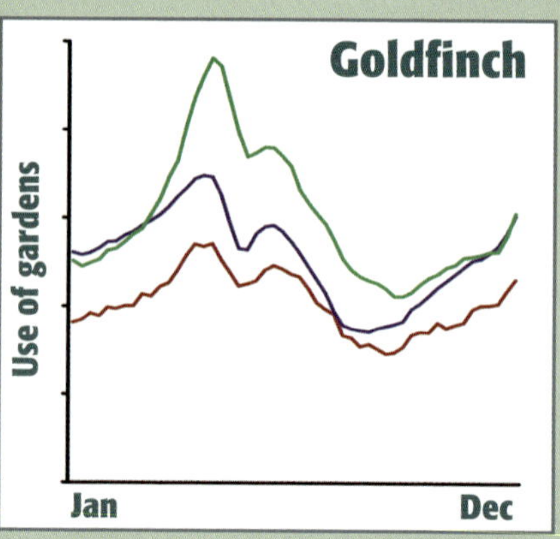

Urban – brown, suburban – blue, rural – green.
Data from the BTO/CJ Garden BirdWatch.

The daily cycle

Spend time watching your bird table first thing in the morning and you will discover that different birds arrive to feed at different times. Blackbirds and Robins are the first birds up and about, while House Sparrows and Greenfinches tend to arrive later, perhaps 30 minutes or more after first light.

Winter: In general, there are three peaks in feeding activity during the day. The first occurs shortly after dawn and is an attempt by individual birds to top-up energy reserves expended keeping warm the previous night. Research shows that Blue Tits may be 5% lighter at dawn than they were on going to roost the previous evening. Since these small birds do not lay down much body fat they need to arrive at feeders early to top-up lost reserves as quickly as possible. Bigger birds, with more reserves, arrive later. Of course, this pattern may be influenced by other factors, such as social dominance or roosting behaviour. A second peak, towards the end of the day, may have a similar function – this time the birds are topping-up before going to roost. A third, smaller, peak occurs in the middle of the day and may be a consequence of competition for food.

Summer: The daily cycle of garden use during the breeding season is also influenced by food availability and energy requirements. However, energy demands change during the breeding season, as birds get into breeding condition, lay down the reserves needed for egg production and seek out food for growing chicks. Many garden birds produce a single egg each day during the period of egg-laying. While female Blue Tits roost in the nest cavity overnight, laying an egg first thing in the morning, Woodpigeons tend to lay their eggs early in the afternoon.

Such birds usually only begin incubation once all the eggs have been laid and you may well notice the absence of your regular female Blackbird while she is tucked away incubating. Once there are youngsters in the nest, both parents will spend a lot of time looking for suitable food, usually invertebrates, and so you may see them visiting the flowers, shrubs and trees in search of potential prey. Activity at hanging feeders is likely to diminish at this time, increasing again later in the season as parent birds bring their newly fledged chicks to learn about the easy food on offer.

Juvenile Starling – Christine M Matthews

Seasonal Patterns

The comings and goings of birds vary with season and are more obvious for some species than others. The winter arrival of Bramblings or Waxwings is obvious because such birds do not normally breed here but the arrival of immigrant Blackbirds and Chaffinches is less obvious because you cannot tell them apart from resident individuals.

Male Brambling – John Harding

A number of general patterns can be seen in the seasonality of garden use by resident birds. Most pronounced is the distinct trough seen in the autumn. This is a time of the year when, with breeding over, many birds undergo their annual moult and become secretive. They also make use of the autumn bounty of fruits and seeds, typically leaving gardens to forage in other habitats (such as woodland and farmland). Such is the scale of departure from gardens that many garden birdwatchers worry that something has happened to their birds.

Some species, for example Great Spotted Woodpecker and Jackdaw, show a peak in garden use during the early part of the summer. In the case of the Jackdaw, this ties in with the period when the adults have the most difficulty in finding sufficient food for growing chicks. In the case of the woodpeckers it matches the period when they bring recently-fledged young to feed at hanging feeders.

The use of Gardens

An autumn trough in the use of gardens by species like Blackbird may alarm some observers but it is easily explained by the fact that these birds are making use of autumn's bounty by feeding elsewhere.

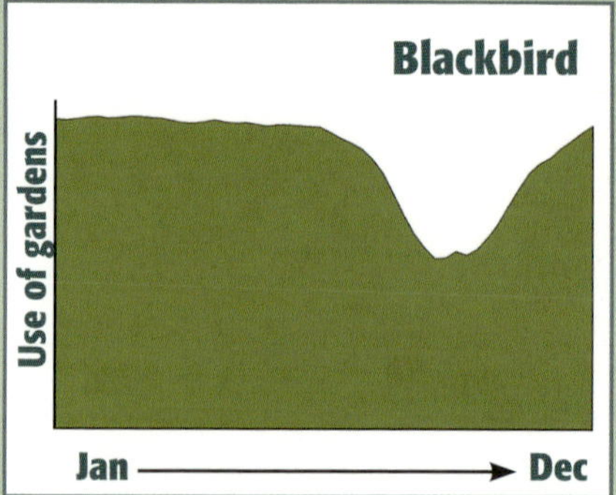

Great Spotted Woodpeckers make greatest use of gardens in early-summer, when they bring their youngsters to feeding stations.

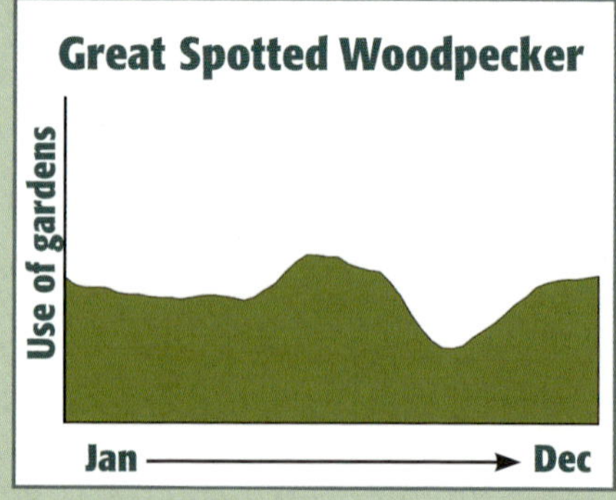

Garden for birds

Gardens, then, are important for birds and a range of different species can be expected to visit most gardens. Knowing how birds use gardens, and which features are important to them, should enable you to develop your own garden in a way that makes it more attractive to as wide a range of species as possible. Gardening for birds is also about providing features for other wildlife, especially insects, since most birds are dependent upon these other creatures for food. Take up the challenge and garden!

GARDEN BASICS

Working with nature

A garden that is good for wildlife is likely to be a stable ecosystem in its own right, integrated with the landscape around it and providing a diversity of micro-habitats within its bounds. Such stability has advantages for you, the gardener, as well. A stable, diverse system is unlikely to be over-dominated by any one species or group of organisms. In practical terms this means that you should have fewer problems with pest or weed species and be less prone to outbreaks of disease amongst the plants that you grow.

Gatekeeper – Mike Toms

Working with nature should also reduce the amount of management work that you have to do within the garden – something which can prove invaluable in our increasingly busy lives. The concept of working with nature is rooted in a number of guiding principles, each of which should underpin the development of your garden for wildlife. Let us look at some of these.

Integrate with the landscape – As
highlighted in the preceding chapter, the range of species that uses your garden depends, in a large part, on where your garden is located and by which habitats it is surrounded. It is important, therefore, to consider the surrounding landscape before setting about adding features to your garden. You may not be able to provide a feature that a particular species needs in order to breed but you may be able to add a feature that supports the species if it happens to be breeding somewhere nearby.

For example, the Gatekeeper butterfly does not usually breed in gardens because it needs areas of tall rank grasses for egg-laying. While such micro-habitats are still to be found in farmland, often alongside hedgerows, nectar sources important to the adults may well be missing. If you live in a rural location, you could boost the local Gatekeeper population by providing the missing nectar sources. This can be done through planting Wild Marjoram *Origanum vulgare*, Common Fleabane *Pulicaria dysenterica* or bramble *Rubus fruticosus* agg.

Provide plenty of choice – Any species
using your garden will be looking for one or more of the resources it requires to satisfy basic needs. These can best be summarised as food, water, shelter and a place to breed. These four requirements may not all be found within the same habitat and it is for this reason that many species are migratory, moving between areas that meet their different needs at particular times of the year. As gardeners, we are in the privileged position of being able to create an artificially high number of habitats, or micro-habitats, within a small area. A Blackbird, for example, may nest and shelter in your shrubs, feed on worms taken from your lawn or bathe in your pond. Such features are surrogates for the naturally-occurring micro-habitats found within the woodland shrub layer and woodland glades.

With careful planning, it should be possible to create a whole host of different micro-habitats within your garden, meeting the resource requirements of a wide range of species. Given that the vast bulk of the wildlife that is going to be using your garden will be very small in size, many of these micro-habitats can themselves be small; for example, a warm south-facing bank in a sheltered part of the garden or a small pile of logs tucked up against the back of a shed. It is not too difficult to create parts of the garden that are damp or dry, sunny or shaded, to have vegetation of different heights, growth forms, colours or flowering periods. Pull it all together and you have something that is rather special.

Plant origins: native versus alien –
The communities of plants growing within our gardens are likely to be rather different from those established in other habitats. A typical garden flora will almost certainly be composed of a mixture of native and non-native (alien) species, selected for a range of reasons not necessarily linked to their wildlife benefit. Therefore, when planning a garden for wildlife, it is essential to think about the reasons why you wish to use a particular flower or shrub and to seek advice on its wildlife value (see later chapters).

There has been a significant amount written about the benefits of using native species in preference to alien ones. However, in contrast to the plethora of advice derived from the notion that native plants *are* good for wildlife and introduced ones *are* bad, there has been very little scientific research into this particular question. That which has been done, notably including a 1961 paper by Southwood, has sometimes been interpreted incorrectly. This has, for instance, led to alien species, such as Sycamore, being dismissed out of hand. However, the paper in question was based on very incomplete information for introduced tree species and there was uncertainty about the attribution of species records to particular tree species within a genus. It may turn out that alien species may support more species than was initially apparent.

The degree to which a particular plant (native or otherwise) is useful to an organism will depend on exactly what the organism is looking to get from the plant. If the organism is just using some structural or architectural feature of the plant then the chances are that it matters little if the plant is native or introduced. However, if the organism seeks to feed on the plant then the plant's origin may become important. This is because the chemistry of the plant may be different from that seen in the native species alongside which the organism has evolved.

Alien flowers may prove unsuitable for native insects either because they are unattractive (not giving off the right signal), unprofitable (not delivering sufficient rewards) or inaccessible (not providing the right shaped access). This mismatch can occur if the introduced plants have evolved to attract and service pollinators very different from our own. For example, even though the Scarlet Sage *Salvia splendens* produces plenty of nectar, the shape of its flowers means that this nectar is inaccessible to even the longest-tongued bumblebees. In its native South American range, Scarlet Sage is pollinated by hummingbirds. There is some evidence, though, that the small bee *Apis mellifera* is able to pollinate this plant.

Interestingly, alien plant species grown in British gardens mainly come from plant families with representatives already native to our shores. Since the chemistry of individual plant species is typically similar within a family, plant-feeding insects should (in many cases) be able to quickly adapt to feeding on introduced species. Research carried out as part of Sheffield University's *Biodiversity in Urban Gardens* project has shown that alien species dominate the garden flora – the 61 Sheffield gardens studied contained 1,166 plant species, 70% of which were alien. Yet, at the family level, just 36% of the families were alien in origin. This again suggests that herbivorous insects should be able to exploit many of the alien species planted in our gardens.

There are plenty of examples of native invertebrates moving onto introduced tree and shrub species; for example more than 70 species of plant-feeding moth have been recorded feeding on *Nothofagus nervosa*, a species of introduced beech from the southern hemisphere. There are even instances of native species (for example the Pine Beauty Moth) becoming pests on introduced plants. Conversely, there are cases where a non-native moth has been able to colonise Britain through the introduction of an alien plant; examples include Blair's Shoulder Knot on Leyland Cypress and Firethorn Leaf Miner on *Pyracantha*.

Of course, there are other reasons why planting natives may be preferable to planting aliens. Globally, the harmful effect of alien species on local ecosystems is regarded as one of the greatest threats to biological diversity and, closer to home, there are a number of high profile instances where introduced plants have caused major conservation problems. Rhododendron *Rhododendron ponticum*, New Zealand Pigmyweed *Crassula helmsii*, Japanese Knotweed *Fallopia japonica* and Himalayan Balsam *Impatiens glandulifera* have all hit the headlines in recent years. The negative impact of invasive aliens is likely to be even more of an issue in countries with a high component of endemics (*e.g.* Tasmania). Ironically, New Zealand Pigmyweed was introduced to Britain in 1911 from Tasmania!

Urban pond – Mike Toms

While it would be fair to say that there has been little direct comparison of native and alien species and their use by insects and other organisms, it would be wrong to say that alien plants as a whole have little or no wildlife value. Some will be of value (urban butterfly populations in California are entirely dependent upon introduced plants), some will not be of value and some will be invasive and should be avoided altogether. Those producing nectar (particularly at times of year when there may be few native nectar producers available) or those providing berries, fruits or seeds, can be especially useful and should be considered to fill gaps in native planting schemes. More information on specific plant choices (native or otherwise) can be found on pages 61 to 76.

Our own preference, and that used in planting the BTO Nunnery Garden, is to use species of local provenance where possible – *i.e.* not just native but known to grow locally and sourced from stocks/ suppliers of known provenance. Alien species were used where appropriate and where there was a clear wildlife benefit. Of course, these were personal decisions and you may well adopt a different approach. The Postcode Plants database (http://www.nhm.ac.uk/fff/) provides a great starting point for finding which plants grow locally around your property.

Flower form – There is an ever-increasing array of plant varieties on sale at garden centres and specialist nurseries these days, with new colour forms and structurally divergent cultivars of familiar plants available for use in our gardens. Such cultivars may be very variable in their wildlife value when compared with ancestral forms. For example, the double cultivars of certain species have been popular because of their novel appearance and because of their longer flowering season. However, these double cultivars have been shown to produce less seed (reducing their value for seed-eating insects) and their unusual structure may also decrease their value to nectar-feeding species of invertebrates.

Researchers at the University of Cambridge demonstrated for Bird's-foot-trefoil *Lotus corniculatus* that, while the single Bird's-foot-trefoil produced both nectar and pollen – well exploited by insects, the double form 'Plenus' failed to provide either pollen or nectar. Similarly, the double cultivar 'Rose Duo' of *Petunia* x *hybrida* contained virtually no nectar and was useless for insects. Yet the same authors found that in the Asteraceae (*Tagetes* and *Calendula*) a degree of doubling had very little effect on the number of visiting insects.

With this in mind, try to plant a mixture of plants with different flowering structures. With their short tongues, honeybees, hoverflies and some of the bumblebees can only reach the nectar in plants with short flower tubes. The longer-tongued bumblebees and butterflies can access the hard-to-reach nectar tucked away at the end of a long flower tube. Again, use the guidelines on pages 70 to 76 to help select plants and varieties for particular roles within your garden. With a little planning you can please a wide range of invertebrates!

Don't be too tidy-minded – The

traditional autumn clean-up, such a prominent part of the gardening calendar for many gardeners, robs much beneficial wildlife of crucial overwintering sites. In addition, the removal of dead seed heads, such as Teasel *Dipsacus fullonum*, takes away food sources that are readily exploited by finches. If you can leave at least some of these resources then the wildlife will benefit. If stands of spent flowerheads are not to your taste, try to adopt an attitude of 'enlightened untidiness', clearing debris only from the most prominent parts of the garden and leaving the out of the way bits untouched through into spring.

Encourage decay – A very tidy

garden also impacts on the natural recycling of nutrients, notably by removing dead material to the council tip. Many insects and other organisms make a living out of breaking down dead material, extracting nutrients and, by doing so, free these up again for the garden food chain. Try to recycle plant material within the garden by creating your own compost heap and/or, better still, promote some recycling *in situ*. This can be done by using dead plant material as a mulch, though remembering to remove the seeds of aggressive weeds. The mulch will provide an added bonus by reducing water loss from around newly established plants during the dry summer months and will also suppress weed growth.

Avoid unnecessary chemicals

– It is easy to reach for one of the many herbicides, fungicides or insecticides when managing your garden. The problem is that most of these compounds don't just tackle a problem species but also impact on the other plants and animals within the garden and, as such, may imbalance the equilibrium that you were trying to establish in the first place. Once your garden becomes established many pest-related problems settle down without the need for intervention. Admittedly, newly-created gardens may prove to be more problematic and a glyphosate herbicide may be the best way to clear an area for replanting.

It is worth considering various plant husbandry techniques (for example, companion planting) or organic alternatives for dealing with specific pests and diseases. Some varieties or species are more disease resistant than others; for instance, while the New England Aster *Aster novae-angliae* can suffer from mildew, *Aster x frikartii* seems untroubled and may be a useful replacement (we'd recommend *Aster x frikartii* 'Wunder von Stäfa' with its long-lasting blue flowers and stout stems). There are other suggestions for tackling specific problems throughout this book.

Enjoy your garden – You should

seek to enjoy your garden – not just the end result but the creative process of developing the garden and adding new features with specific aims in mind. A garden is never finished but is an entity that develops and changes over time. This is why gardening is such an absorbing and pleasurable pastime.

Enhance an existing garden

– The chances are that, if you are reading this book, you will already have an established garden and won't have a completely blank canvas on which to layout your new wildlife-friendly garden.

Corncockle – Mike Toms

However, it is quite likely that you will also have some aspect of your existing garden that you are not completely happy with, that you wish to enhance and make more favourable for wildlife.

With this in mind, much of this book is devoted to features and ideas that can be incorporated into an already established garden. Before we get to grips with these, we need to look at the basics of selecting plants, planting techniques and garden maintenance.

Selecting plants

The previous section on working with nature will have already given you some idea of how to go about selecting suitable plants, choosing those that offer particular wildlife benefits, have long flowering seasons or which are to be found in local habitats. However, there are other practicalities to consider.

Perhaps the most important of these is to ensure that the plant you select for a particular spot in the garden is going to be happy there. To be sure of this, you need to know what conditions the plant in question favours; does it like acidic or alkaline soil, heavy or light conditions, sun or shade? This also means that you need to know about the condition of your soil and the microclimates within the garden itself. This may seem obvious but, speaking from experience, it is easy to be seduced by convincing displays at garden centres and to come home with a plant that is never going to do well in your garden. If the growing conditions are not suitable then a plant will not thrive and will become more susceptible to pests or diseases. This is another reason why selecting plants known to grow locally can make a big difference.

Clearly then, you need to think about what you want to achieve before you start, even if it is just adding some new, wildlife-friendly plants to an existing bed. A simple sketch plan can help, especially if you want to get an idea of how the colours will work together or need to calculate the number of plants required. Read up on the plants you

Soil types

Sandy soils – These are free-draining and easy to work. However, since they do not retain moisture well (a problem in itself), soil nutrients quickly leach away. Adding a degree of organic material can improve soil condition and a mulch can be particularly useful during the summer to help reduce moisture loss.

Clay soils – Sticky when wet and hard when dry, these soils can be very difficult to work. They do, however, hold on to nutrients (and release them slowly) which is good for the plants. Avoid walking on or working them when wet and only add organic matter as a mulch or to the top 15 cm of soil.

Silty soils – These soils tend to be deep and fertile, holding water well. Mind you, if too wet or if heavily trampled they can become compacted and airless; too dry and they turn to dust. Organic matter, both as mulch and dug into the soil, is useful for maintaining soil structure.

Peaty soils – Such soils are often rich in organic matter and are easy to work. However, they can become very dry in summer and wet in winter. Importantly, many such soils are only really suitable for acid-loving plants.

Chalky soils – Chalky soils are usually quite shallow in profile and full of lumps of chalk and/or flint. They have a high pH and so favour alkaline-loving plants. Being relatively free-draining they have a high demand for water and nutrients.

Urban garden – Mike Toms

are thinking about incorporating into your plan (for example, by using the lists elsewhere in this book) and sketch out where you want to place them. The border plans drawn from the BTO's Nunnery Garden may provide a starting point, with each one targeted towards particular growing conditions, but there is nothing to stop you adding to them, changing them or reworking them completely with your own ideas.

You will almost certainly need to put some time into preparing the ground, perhaps even enhancing the quality of your soil, before you start out. Time spent on such work is almost invariably worthwhile. It also gives you a chance to think in more detail about the design and to visualise it before you make a financial commitment to the plants themselves.

Once you are happy with the design, then it is time to purchase the plants. These can be purchased as seeds, young plugs or older plants and there are advantages and disadvantages to each of these different sources. Establishing plants from seed (or from cuttings) can be a very rewarding process; it can also be quite time consuming and it may be easier to establish some plants by buying them in from a local nursery. We adopted this approach for many of the perennials used in the BTO Nunnery Garden. Other plants, notably those used in the lawn and wildflower mixtures were established from seed.

Take time to source the plants that you want, and don't feel restricted to the stock available in your local garden centre. There are many nurseries nationally which cater for gardeners seeking the sorts of plants more suited to a wildlife-friendly garden. It is now increasingly easy and convenient to browse nursery lists over the Internet and to mail order your plants.

Planting techniques

There are two general rules when establishing a border. The first is to place taller plants at the back of the border, the second to plant individuals in small odd-numbered groups. The resulting effect is easy on the eye, looking more natural (less regimented), and provides the sort of vertical and spatial diversity that offers the greatest benefits to a wide range of wildlife.

Know your soil – the importance of chemistry

Understanding the nature of your soil is important and a basic understanding of soil chemistry can prove really useful when it comes to selecting plants. One of the most important elements is the pH of the soil – a measure of the degree of acidity or alkalinity. Most plants, including fruit and vegetables, will grow within a pH range that extends from 5.5 to 7.5 but there are some that favour more acidic soils while others favour more alkaline conditions. Test your soil by using one of the commercially available kits and then select plants accordingly.

Soil structure – Mike Toms

You also need to consider the colour, shape and form of the plants that you are adding in order to ensure that you have produced something that is visually appealing. From a purely wildlife point of view such considerations may be less important (though colour and form may have a bearing on the degree to which a plant is used by a particular type of insect). However, you should certainly think about providing a successional interest by planting species that have variable flowering seasons or which offer different resources at different times of the year.

Once you have selected the plants and prepared your soil, by digging it over and removing any weeds, position your new plants (still in their containers) to see how the planting will come together. Planting requirements vary with plant type and are best summarised as follows:

Perennials – If purchased as container plants, these may be planted out at any time of the year when the soil is workable. However, between autumn and spring is best, with the autumn conditions allowing plants to establish quickly in the

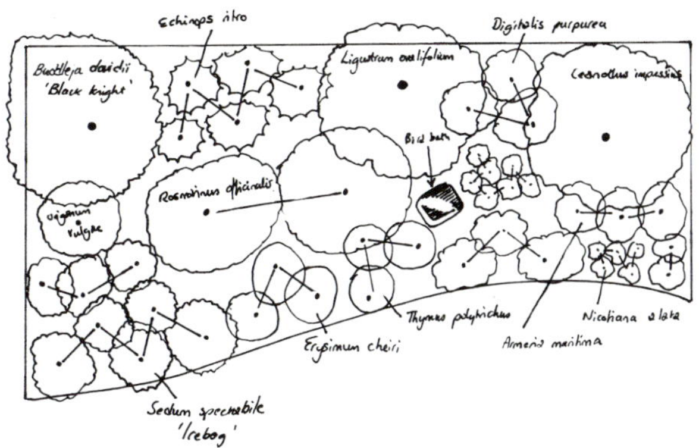

A simple sketch can help you visualise the final layout for your border.

still warm soil without drying out. Spring planting may be preferable in those areas of the country where the winter months bring hard frost or result in wet ground. The earlier one can plant in the autumn-winter-spring sequence, the longer the establishment time the plant's roots have to develop before the dry summer. Some plants, such as *Scabiosa caucasica* do much better with spring planting.

Bare-root sourced perennials can be planted from autumn to spring, though avoid periods when the soil may be waterlogged. They should be planted in a hole that is roughly one and a half times wider and deeper than the root ball, having first been soaked in a bucket of water for a short period.

Plants can even be moved from one part of the garden to another (i.e. essentially bare-root) if necessary in summer, so long as regular watering is possible. In this case cutting back much of the plant's foliage can help survival, even at the expense of that year's flowers.

The planting depth is typically set so that the plant is flush with the soil surface. Plants that prefer moist conditions (such as *Hosta*) should be set just below ground level, while those prone to rotting (e.g. *Sisyrinchium*) should be planted slightly raised above ground level to improve drainage around the crown.

Recognise a healthy plant

If purchasing container-grown plants (typically perennials), look for those that have a small number of strong healthy shoots with a few buds, rather than those with a larger number of weak buds. Also look for signs that the plant is healthy – strong bright top growth, a well-established root system and growing in moist compost.

Avoid plants that look under-developed, that are in dry compost or that have a root system that is pot-bound. The presence of mosses or liverworts in the pot is usually a sign that the plant has been in the pot for too long, and that the soil is waterlogged and lacking in nutrients.

Trees and shrubs – Container-grown specimens can be planted following the same guidelines as given for perennials, Bare-root specimens are normally available (and should be planted) from autumn through into spring, during what is their dormant period. Trees and shrubs should be planted into a hole that is 2–4 times as wide as the diameter of the root ball, into which is dug well-rotted organic matter. Large trees and shrubs generally need staking but remember to place the stake in the hole first to avoid damaging the delicate roots.

Starting from seed – Growing things from seed not only gives you a real sense of achievement but can also save you money. This approach can require a degree of patience and knowledge of the seed's particular requirements. Fortunately, most packets of seed come with detailed instructions on what you need to do to germinate the plant.

Many seeds will establish themselves with relative ease; you simply need to prepare the seed bed, sow the seeds and then let nature do its thing.

Others need more attention, perhaps being raised indoors in a propagator or a greenhouse to get them started, before being transplanted later on into their final position within your garden.

Avoid the temptation to sow your seeds too early in the year; most seeds will not germinate if the soil temperature is below 7°C and the longer they remain in such cold, damp soil, the more likely they are to be attacked by pests. A few seeds actually need a period of cold before they will germinate and a number of native species (including Holly *Ilex aquifolium*, Hawthorn *Crataegus monogyna* and Cowslip *Primula veris*) should be sown in seed trays in the autumn and then left *in situ* over winter, either outside or in a cold frame.

Other options – Many plants and shrubs can be propagated by division or from cuttings, the latter taken either from stems (e.g. *Buddleja*, *Delphinium*, *Achillea* and *Erysimum*), roots (*Eryngium* and *Papaver*) or leaves (*Begonia*). Division is particularly useful for reinvigorating older perennials.

Achillea fillipendulina 'Gold Plate' – Mike Toms

Ongoing maintenance

All gardens require a certain amount of ongoing maintenance in order to keep them developing in the right direction. Some aspects require more maintenance than others but in all cases there should be a clear objective involved (for example, removing lawn clippings to reduce soil fertility).

Mulching – Covering the ground with a layer of mulch serves three functions. First, the mulch acts to reduce water loss through evaporation; second, it helps prevent weeds from establishing and, third, it can alter the temperature just above the ground surface – something that may promote plant growth.

Organic, biodegradable mulches are best, improving soil structure and supplying plants with additional nutrients. These enter the soil through the community of decomposer organisms, which break the mulch down and make the nutrients more widely available. A mulch (such as that provided by leaf mould, compost, well-rotted manure, lawn mowings or chipped wood) is best used in a layer that is at least one inch in depth. This will provide the desired water retention benefits but a thicker layer (say four inches) is needed if the aim is to prevent weed establishment. It is best to leave a gap around the base of each plant so that it does not become damp and subject to rot or disease. Think about where and why you want to use a mulch and avoid using an organic mulch if you do not want to increase the fertility of your soil. Other mulches should be avoided under certain conditions – *e.g.* it has been suggested that cocoa shell mulches may be toxic to dogs. Mushroom compost may increase soil alkalinity.

Pruning – Perhaps the commonest reason for pruning is to maintain balance within the border, preventing the bullies from taking over by controlling their growth rate and size. Geoff Hamilton called this 'umpiring'. Pruning can also encourage desired growth. Aims can be the aesthetic ones of shape or size, or can be more practical, where the future wellbeing or productivity of the plant is involved. Thinning to open the canopy to let in more air and light, preventing crossing branches (which can lead to rubbing and disease entry), or removing dead or dying tissue to prevent disease spread are all concerns here. Of course, for the bird gardener, it is important to provide nesting sites and shelter, so we can find ourselves perversely creating additional branching and a closed, dense structure! Pruning can also be used to increase flowering and fruiting, good for both the gardener and many birds.

All cuts should be made with sharp tools; secateurs for shoots and smaller branches and loppers or a pruning saw for larger ones. Always try to cut back to just above a healthy bud to prevent die-back of the tissue below the cut. Outward facing buds will encourage the plant to branch in that direction and develop an attractive open structure, whereas inward facing ones will form a more bird-friendly denser plant; it's your choice, although different shrub species vary in their ideal look, of course. Don't cut larger branches right back to the trunk but leave the collar where the two meet intact. An initial cut beneath the branch will prevent a strip of bark tearing off down the trunk. Covering the cut with wound paint is no longer considered necessary.

How and when to prune a *Buddleja*

Buddleja davidii is a vigorous plant and requires fairly drastic pruning to encourage flowering. The extent of the pruning depends, in part on where the bush is located – those at the back of a bed should be pruned back to a framework of about 3–4 ft height, while those further forward in a bed should be cut to no more than 2 ft height.

During the first spring after planting, the main stems need to be shortened to roughly two-thirds of their length, pruning just above a pair of buds. In subsequent springs, cut back the previous season's growth and look to see if any of the older growth needs to be removed to reduce congestion. The timing of the prune will influence when the Buddleja will flower; pruning later into the spring will delay flowering, so it is possible to produce a succession of flowering across several plants by pruning one in January, one in February, one in March and one in early April. Note that not all Buddlejas should be treated the same (see text)!

For most species, the harder a plant is pruned the more vigorously it will grow back. Light pruning will encourage slower but more branching growth. These principles can be used for many trees and shrubs to reshape an uneven specimen by cutting the weak side back hard but the stronger side lightly. In apples/pears pruning selected shoots lightly will promote the development of fruiting spurs. Many hopelessly overgrown and distorted shrubs can be rejuvenated by cutting right back (coppicing) to within a few inches of the base. The new young growth can then be managed to the desired form as it develops. Feeding helps considerably; dogwoods (*Cornus*), *Berberis*, and Hazel (*Corylus*) are good examples. Major cutting back of deciduous shrubs should be carried out any time during the dormant winter season but evergreens are best left until late winter or early spring, so they can photosynthesise earlier in the winter.

Shrubs flower either on new (this season's) or old (last season's) growth. Those flowering on new wood should be pruned in early spring, allowing the flowers to develop afterwards. *Buddleja davidii* (the butterfly bush), *Caryopteris*, and fuchsia are in this group. Species flowering on old wood should be pruned immediately after the previous year's

flowering; if left until winter or spring this year's flower buds will be removed. *Buddleja globosa*, *Philadelphus*, and Jasmine (*Jasminum*) fall into this category. Not all shrubs need pruning – if there's room, then why not let some grow to their full potential with their natural shape? The extra height and leaf area will provide more caterpillars and other invertebrates for birds, moths for bats, and will benefit the whole garden. Alternatively, a natural shape and some height can be kept by removing, say, a fifth of the oldest and largest branches each year. Over five years the whole plant will be replenished.

Most pruning of perennials involves tidying up and cutting back at the end of the year. If possible leave the end of the year tidy-up until spring, to leave seeds on the plants for birds and hollow stems and other dead vegetation for invertebrate overwintering. This also applies to the smaller shrubs such as lavenders, which can reward you with Goldfinches feeding on the seed-heads at Christmas if you don't clip until spring.

Climbers that form permanent structures tend to be better for wildlife, providing overwintering shelter and nest sites. These usually only require light pruning after flowering, using secateurs or even shears to control overall growth.

For further advice on individual species refer to the excellent books on pruning produced by the RHS.

Pests and disease – The organic approach to dealing with pests and diseases is the one that we have chosen to adopt for the BTO Nunnery Garden. Such an approach is directed at the whole garden, the aim being to prevent a problem occurring in the first place, by keeping pest and disease populations at a manageable level. This is best done through the encouragement of natural enemies and a management approach that reduces the risk factors associated with particular diseases. The fundamental requirement of this approach is to maintain healthy plants by planting them in the right place and by ensuring that they receive the required amounts of water and nutrients. Healthy, vigorous plants will be less susceptible to disease than those that are stressed.

Prevention is better than cure and there are a number of steps that you can take to reduce the risk of future problems. These are:

i) consider planting cultivars that show some resistance to diseases more widely associated with the species,

ii) inspect or even quarantine all new plants to reduce the chances of bringing a disease or pest into the garden,

iii) maintain diversity and avoid monocultures/high stocking densities,

iv) consider companion planting – for instance, establishing four rows of onions to each row of carrots will protect against Carrot Root Fly for as long as the onion leaves are growing; strong smelling alliums are reputed to reduce the occurrence of blackspot on nearby roses.

v) remove and destroy infected material as soon as you find it.

Finally, be pragmatic and give in gracefully if you cannot find a solution to a particular pest or disease problem; you can always try a different approach next year. It is worth remembering that a

The hoverfly *Volucella zonaria* – Graham Jarvis

pest is only a pest because we deem that it has interfered with our own activities. So, it is well worth assessing the actual degree of impact before jumping straight to the conclusion that the 'pest' needs to be removed. Pest species are part of the food chain and provide a resource to be exploited by other organisms; remove them completely and you remove part of the food web. Even worse, remove them with an insecticide and the chances are that the insecticide will also remove other 'non-target' organisms, further upsetting the balance that you are trying to achieve.

If you decide that a particular pest needs to be controlled through direct intervention (rather than through crop husbandry techniques) then you have various options, ranging from the chemical (insecticides), through the mechanical (trapping or collecting the pest by hand) to the biological (using biological control agents – typically predators or parasites of the species that you wish to control).

Some of the biological control agents can be used effectively only within the greenhouse environment but others (notably those for slug and Vine Weevil control) can be used outside with a good degree of success. It is worth noting that biological control agents are not without risk, since some have gone on to become pests in their own right by attacking other non-target species.

Vine Weevil

Although the adults of this species inflict largely cosmetic damage to a range of plants, their larvae can do some serious damage to plants, especially those established in containers. The subterranean larvae eat away at the root system, causing the plant to wilt and die. Since the Vine Weevil cannot fly, individual plants can be protected by using a band of non-drying glue around the pot or stand. A biological control agent, the parasitic nematode *Heterorhabditis megidis*, can be used against the larvae. This is best applied late in the summer when the soil temperature is above 10°C.

Slugs & snails

While isolated beds can be protected with a water-filled moat, this is not an effective method for other areas of the garden. Various materials are marketed as slug barriers; most of these are composed of a porous material that the slugs find unpleasant to cross. If the material becomes damp it loses its effectiveness. In addition, slugs will quite happily move under the soil to bypass a barrier. A battery-powered electrical barrier has been developed that slugs will not pass; there are also copper bands that work in a similar way by setting up a small static charge around the pot. These can be purchased in tape form, making them easy to apply to a clean pot. A simple slug trap, made from a container full of stale beer – the lip set just above the soil surface to prevent non-target species entering – works particularly well, as does hand-picking at night by torch-light. Hand-picking has the advantage that slugs and snails can be relocated elsewhere if desired. A nematode treatment, using *Phasmarhabditis hermaphrodita* can also be used outside for slugs.

Slug-resistant plants

There are various plants that appear less palatable to slugs and snails. These can be grown in those parts of the garden where levels of slug and snail damage may previously have been high, perhaps because it is a damp or shady corner. Alternatively, these plants can be incorporated into borders where other more sensitive plants are positioned, hiding the degree of damage inflicted.

Slug-resistant plants are more likely to have hairy or succulent leaves, while big fleshy leaves (like those of *Hosta* spp.) are favoured. Interestingly, hostas with thicker, more leathery leaves tend to suffer less slug and snail damage and several hosta specialists list resistant varieties (Bond 1997).

The following plants have all been found to be less palatable to slugs and snails: *Acanthus mollis, Achillea filipendulina, Aquilegia* spp., *Centaurea montana, Digitalis purpurea, Liatris spicata, Linaria vulgaris, Nepeta* x *faassenii, Phlox paniculata, Scabiosa caucasica, Sedum spectabile, Stachys macrantha* and *Verbascum* spp.

Whatever you attempt in your garden, always start by planning what you are going to do. Understand the basics of how plants grow, ensure you know what to look for when choosing a plant for a particular spot and find out about potential pests and diseases. By getting the basics right, you are well on the road to developing the problem-free garden that you are after.

There are plenty of excellent books out there, providing additional information on virtually every topic. There are also web sites and discussion groups where wildlife gardeners share their expertise, highlighting what has worked and what has failed. Our resources section (pages 89 to 92) should point you in the right direction.

DESIGN ELEMENTS

The key to a successful wildlife-friendly garden is its design; the range of features that you include and the way that these fit together. Of course, the chances are that you are not starting from a blank canvas with your own garden, rather you have an existing design that you wish to add new, wildlife-friendly, features to. This may mean the addition of a new flowerbed (or the replacement of an existing one), the creation of a pond or a change in the way in which you manage your lawn.

This section of the book presents a series of design features, together with suggested planting schemes, in an effort to provide you with the ideas and tools that you need to enhance your garden. All of these features will require some forethought, thinking about placement within your garden, together with an understanding of what is possible; you can't, for instance, hope to establish a border full of sun-loving plants attractive to butterflies by placing it in the dampest, most heavily shaded part of your garden. For this reason, we have divided up this section into smaller parts, each dealing with a particular set of features and each largely geared towards certain environmental conditions. We start by looking at a flowerbed, planted with species attractive to insects, and then go on to cover the tricky subject of lawns, before expanding to cover a range of other interesting features.

A border for insects

If it is to prove attractive to a wide range of insects, a flower border should contain a diverse mix of plants, drawn from a range of families and with different flowering periods and growth forms. It should also be placed in that part of the garden where it is sheltered from the wind but, at the same time, catches the sun (sunny and south-facing is the key phrase here). This combination of warmth and shelter will suit winged insects like bumblebees, hoverflies and butterflies. You should also consider adding plants that are particularly attractive to moths, on the wing while you are tucked up in bed. These might include Common Evening-primrose *Oenothera biennis*, Night-scented Stock

Traditional garden with lawn, flowery lawn, pond (fenced to protect from ducks while establishing) and butterfly mound – Mike Toms

Matthiola longipetala subsp. *bicornis*, Common Jasmine *Jasmine officinale* and Dame's-violet *Hesperis matronalis*, all of which release much of their fragrance in the evening. The bed should contain perennials, together with some taller shrubs that are normally placed at the back (see page 22) but may be placed along the side to provide shelter from the wind.

Many of the selected plants will act as nectar sources for visiting insects; this is why a mix of flower forms (suited to different insects – see pages 70–76) and flowering times is so important. In particular, try to include some species that provide nectar very early in the season, before other nectar sources become available. Spring-flowering plants (see box, below) will benefit queen bumblebees, newly emerged from hibernation and those butterflies (Peacock, Comma, Brimstone, Small Tortoiseshell and Red Admiral) that overwinter as adults. Detail on which species exploit which plants is given on pages 70–76.

Equally important are those plants which flower late in the summer or through into autumn, since these will enable visiting insects to build up reserves prior to entering hibernation. Again, there are certain species of plant which can be planted within the border to help provide this late season nectar, one of the most important of which very late in the season is Ivy – an ideal plant for any wall or fence that happens to border the back of the flowerbed. See the box below for examples of plants known for their late flowering.

Extending the season of nectar availability

Spring flowering plants

Wallflower *Erysimum cheiri*
Aubretia *Aubrieta deltoidea*
Cuckooflower *Cardamine pratensis*
Lungwort *Pulmonaria officinalis*
Lesser Celandine *Ranunculus ficaria*
Field Forget-me-not *Myosotis arvensis*
Honesty *Lunaria annua*
Primrose *Primula vulgaris*
Dame's-violet *Hesperis matronalis*
Red Clover *Trifolium pratense*
Red Dead-nettle *Lamium purpureum*
Wood Anemone *Anemone nemorosa*
Thrift *Armeria maritima*
Golden Alison *Alyssum saxatilis*
White Dead-nettle *Lamium album*
Daisy *Bellis perennis*
Bluebell *Hyacinthoides non-scripta*
Mahonia x *media* 'winter sun'
Skimmia japonica
Daphne odora

Autumn flowering plants

Buddleja davidii 'Black Knight'
Buddleja x *weyeriana*
Ice Plant *Sedum spectabile*
Greater Knapweed *Centaurea scabiosa*
Lavender *Lavandula angustifolia*
Wild Marjoram *Origanum vulgare*
Thyme *Thymus polytrichus*
Field Scabious *Knautia arvensis*
New England Aster *Aster novi-belgii*
Red Valerian *Centranthus ruber*
Ivy *Hedera helix*

Lungwort *Pulmonaria officinalis* – Mike Toms

Planting scheme for a sunny border

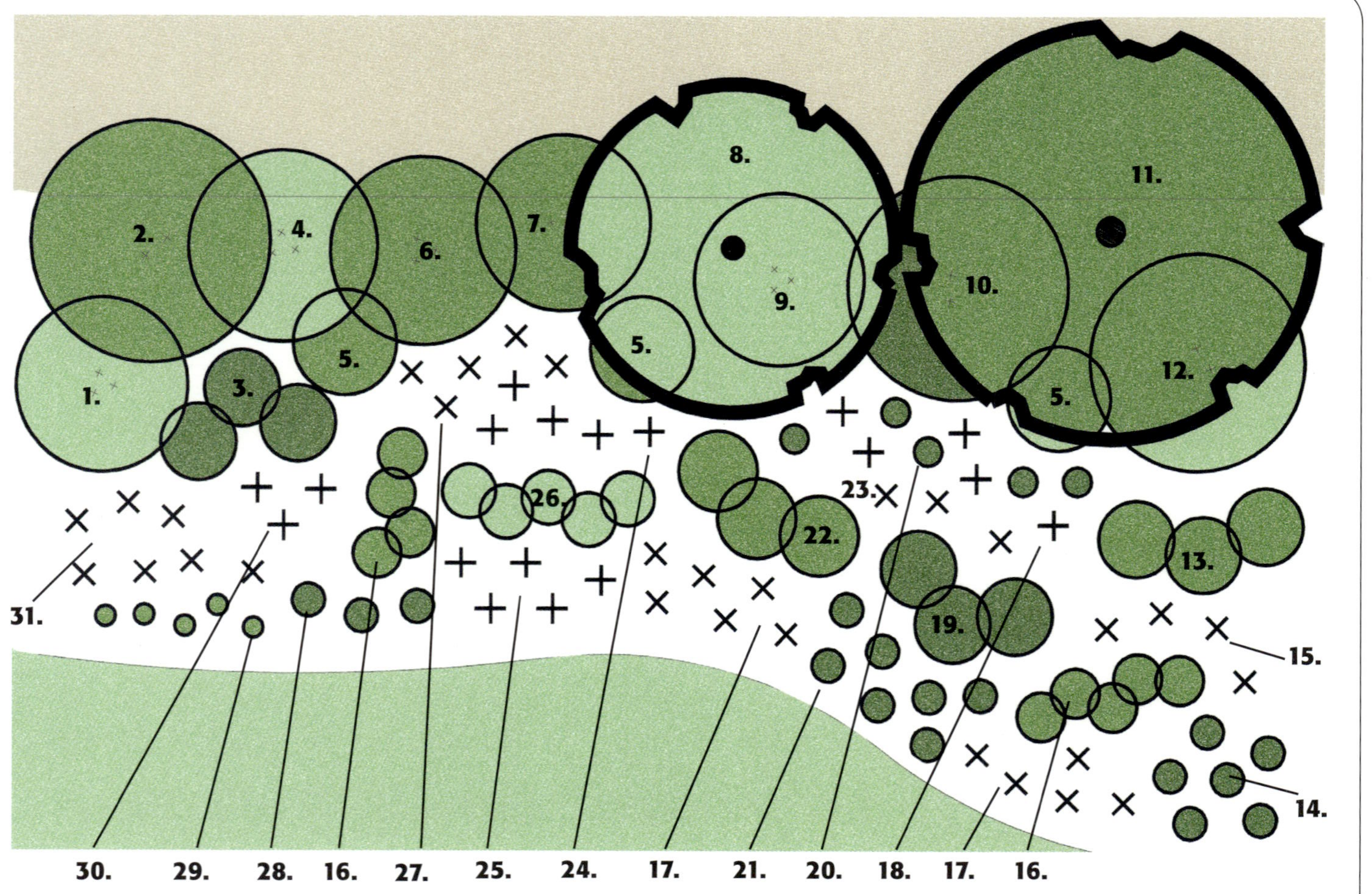

Key to plants used

1. *Hebe* 'Autumn Glory'
2. *Buddleja* x *weyeriana*
3. *Lavandula stoechas*
4. *Syringa microphylla* 'Superba'
5. *Rosemarinus officinalis*
6. *Buddleja davidii* 'Nanho Blue'
7. *Rosa canina*
8. *Malus* 'Red Sentinel'
9. *Pyracantha* 'Saphyr Orange'
10. *Cornus alba* 'Elegantissima'
11. *Cotoneaster cornubia*
12. *Rosa rugosa* 'Alba'
13. *Caryopteris* x *clandonensis* 'Kew Blue'
14. *Origanum vulgare* 'Thumble's Variety'
15. *Centauria scabiosa*
16. *Salvia* x *sylvestris* 'Blauhugel'
17. *Sedum spectabile*
18. *Verbena bonariensis*
19. *Lavandula vera*
20. *Echium vulgare*
21. *Geranium* 'Nimbus'
22. *Hebe albicans* 'Red Edge'
23. *Knautia arvensis*
24. *Aster* x *frikartii* 'Monch'
25. *Nepeta* x *faassenii*
26. *Lavandula angustifolia* 'Twickel Purple'
27. *Verbascum nigrum*
28. *Geranium pratense*
29. *Erysimum* 'Apricot Twist'
30. *Euphorbia myrsinites*
31. *Sedum spectabile* 'Iceberg'

Verbena bonariensis – Mike Toms

Flowery lawn in May, after final spring cut – Mike Toms

Lawns and mini-meadows

For many gardeners, the lawn is the centrepiece of the garden, the place from which we can sit and view the surrounding borders. The image of a bowling green-flat, manicured lawn may be quintessentially English but there is no reason why you cannot develop your lawn into something very different but equally rewarding. From a purely ecological perspective, lawns can appear quite sterile. Plant diversity is kept low by regular mowing and this can have a knock-on impact on the range of invertebrates able to use the lawn. However, there are plants and animals that benefit from the presence of a sward of short grass. Various soil-living invertebrates benefit from elevated soil temperatures and these, in turn, provide food for various birds, like Starlings and Green Woodpeckers.

It is worth noting that 'lawn' and 'meadow' are just terms for different types of grassland, their relative structures largely determined by the management regime employed. In theory, it is possible to 'shift' a lawn towards the more natural looking grassland sward of a meadow by reducing the amount of mowing. However, and here is the rub, this is not something that will happen overnight. The fertility of a typical garden soil favours competitive plant species and these will hinder the sorts of meadow plants that you might wish to establish. Any attempt to create a mini-meadow will almost certainly require some efforts to reduce soil fertility; the creation of such a meadow is dealt with on pages 50 to 53. Here, however, we will deal with the management of more traditional lawns and the creation of flowery lawns.

Traditional lawns

Given the right conditions, grass will grow throughout the year and, as such, a lawn will require its first cut fairly early in the season. This first cut should be set quite high but as the season progresses (and the rate of grass growth increases) the cutting height can be gradually lowered and the frequency of mowing increased. With the season in full swing, aim to remove a third of the growing shoot and cut once, or even twice, a week. Clippings should be removed early in the season, when their bulk may smother the growing shoots and reduce aeration. Later in the season, when the cut is only removing a small amount of material, the clippings can be left, increasing the amount of nitrogen returning to the soil and reducing evaporation. Routine raking is usually carried out in spring (before the first cut) and again in autumn to remove thatch – though note that thatch supports its own community of organisms. Removal of the thatch should promote growth and reduce the build-up of moss. The autumn raking is typically followed by spiking, using a garden fork to create a series of small but deep holes in the lawn will reduce the effects of compaction. Generally, spiking only needs to be done every two to three years but areas of heavy use should be spiked more regularly, possibly as much as once every four to five weeks. Aeration of waterlogged areas can be accomplished by spiking with a hollow-tined tool, removing and replacing the plugs of soil with a dressing of sharp sand and loam. The final autumn job is the top dressing of the lawn proper – using a mix of two parts loam to three parts organic matter (if free-draining) or one part loam to three parts sharp sand and one part fine compost (if wet). This can be applied at a rate of roughly 2kg/m² and worked in well with the back of a rake. Maintaining a lawn is not always easy and there are various problems that may need to be addressed.

Drought – Grass that has ceased growing and turned brown may look unsightly but will regrow once the rain returns. With water resources increasingly in short supply, it is best to accept that the lawn has turned brown rather than waste water in trying to keep it green (a garden sprinkler uses 900 litres of water an hour). A well-looked after lawn withstands drought better than one that is not. Similarly, longer grass tolerates drought better than short.

Watering itself can influence a lawn's ability to withstand drought. Watering lightly early in the summer promotes shallow rooting, making the grass more susceptible to any drought which follows. If you are going to water, make sure that the watering is effective,

soaking the soil down to a depth of 10cm. Don't lose water to evaporation by watering in the heat of the day; early mornings or evenings are better.

Moles – The sight of fresh molehills on a lawn can prove extremely frustrating but once flattened and brushed into the lawn they soon disappear. The problem is that each Mole may produce up to 15 new hills a day, which tends to suggest that it will be an ongoing battle. There are two options when it comes to dealing with Moles. The first, and the only effective solution, is to remove the Moles by trapping, preferably using a live trap (which should be checked at least twice a day). The other approach involves deterrents of various kinds: sonic devices, children's windmills that vibrate in the wind, chemical substances that produce odours, *etc*. Unfortunately, such deterrents only appear to have a limited, short-term effect and the Moles are likely to remain an ongoing problem.

Leatherjackets – These are the larvae of craneflies (daddy long-legs) and feed on the roots of grasses and certain other plants. Since each female lays up to 300 eggs it is easy to see how they can cause areas of lawn to turn yellow and die back. Leatherjackets can be treated with a parasitic nematode (much like

Mole hills – Mike Toms

Wild Pansy – Mike Toms

Vine Weevil – see page 28) or they can be removed by hand. This is done by watering the affected area heavily during the evening and then covering it with a piece of sacking. Come the morning, the sacking can be lifted to reveal leatherjackets that have moved up to the surface because of the water. Leatherjackets are an important food source for Starlings and so their presence in your lawn is not necessarily a bad thing.

Ants – Ants may damage a lawn through the creation of their nests which, like the activities of Moles, may bring aerated soil to the surface. Ants are an important component of natural communities (and provide food for visiting Green Woodpeckers) so are best accepted in a lawn. Once dry, the soil from their nests can be spread across the lawn fairly easily and there is usually no need to reseed the area affected. Many species of ants are sensitive to soil temperature and this is why they tend to make their nests in areas of short-cropped turf.

Suggested plants

Common Bird's-foot Trefoil *Lotus corniculatus*, Bulbous Buttercup *Ranunculus bulbosus*, Common Daisy *Bellis perennis*, Cowslip *Primula veris*, Hoary Plantain *Plantago media*, Lady's Bedstraw *Galium verum*, Red Clover *Trifolium pratense*, Rough Hawkbit *Leontodon hispidus*, Selfheal *Prunella vulgaris*, Wild Pansy *Viola tricolor*.

Flowery lawns

One way to increase the wildlife value of your lawn, without having to go as far as creating a meadow, is to create a flowery lawn. A number of perennials can cope with trampling and regular mowing – except during the flowering period. This sort of lawn is best established from scratch, seeding the area with a mix comprised of 5% wildflower seeds and 95% less-competitive grasses. It is also possible to introduce plants as plugs into an existing lawn but this may not be as successful as starting from scratch. The effectiveness of starting with bare soil can be seen in the Nunnery Garden, where the flowery lawn established very successfully over its first two years.

A traditional lawn (left of the path) and a flowery lawn (right of the path) at the BTO Nunnery Gardens – Mike Toms

Managing a flowery lawn

The flowery lawn created at the BTO Nunnery Garden is mown regularly throughout the year, except between mid-May and mid-July, taking a cut every two weeks and leaving the sward a little longer than you would for a more formal lawn. The regime favours a meadow that flowers in late spring, matching the range of species selected.
The cutting regime that you adopt will have a strong influence on the nature of your flowery lawn because it determines which plants are able to set seed. Mow when a species is still in flower and you will soon lose that plant from your meadow!

Selfheal – Paul Sterry

Hoary Plantain – Andrew Cleave

The right sort of grass

Some grasses are more competitive than others. As such, the ideal grasses to include in a seed mix for a flowery lawn or mini-meadow are those that are less competitive, fine-leaved in nature and native in origin. Avoid those, such as Cock's-foot *Dactylis glomerata* or the various rye grasses *Lolium* spp. which are just too aggressive and stifle diversity. These aggressive species tend to have broad, tough leaves and form large clumps if left uncut. The rye grasses are characterised by their dark green and very shiny leaves. Good species to use include: Meadow Fescue *Festuca pratensis* and Sheep's Fescue *Festuca ovina*. Similarly, before introducing plug plants into an existing grass sward, check to see which grasses are present.

Cowslip – Mike Toms

Grasses – Mike Toms

Sowing your seed

Weed and rake the area to be sown, to form a reasonable tilth. Because wildflower seeds are very fine, you might prefer to mix them with silver sand to help get a decent scatter of seed across the area. A sowing rate of 3-4g/m^2 should do the trick, though seek advice for your particular seed mix. It is best to sow in early autumn since the seeds of some species require a cold spell to break their dormancy. However, you can sow in March or April and accept that some of the seeds won't germinate until the following year. Walk or roll the seeds in and leave them uncovered.

Lady's Bedstraw – Paul Sterry

Planting scheme for a flowery lawn and border

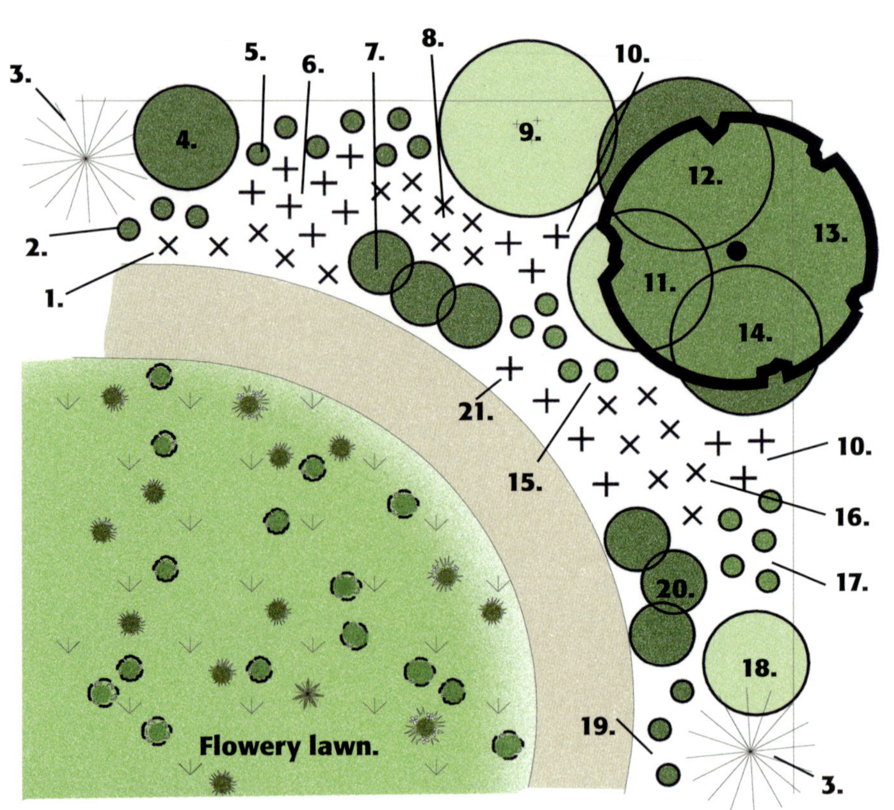

Key to plants used

1. *Geranium pratense* 'Mrs Kendall Clarke'
2. *Erysimum* 'Bowles Mauve'
3. *Stipa gigantea*
4. *Hebe* 'Midsummer Beauty'
5. *Verbascum chaixii*
6. *Hesperis matronalis*
7. *Spiraea japonica* 'Little Princess'
8. *Malva moschata*
9. *Buddleja davidii* 'White Profusion'
10. *Echinops bannaticus* 'Taplow Blue'
11. *Salix lanata*
12. *Ligustrum vulgare*
13. *Betula pendula*
14. *Viburnum burkwoodii*
15. *Achillea filipendula* 'Gold Plate'
16. *Centranthus ruber* 'Albus'
17. *Oenothera fruiticosa*
18. *Senecio* 'Sunshine'
19. *Nepeta* x *faassenii*
20. *Potentilla fruiticosa* 'Abbotswood'
21. *Lavandula angustifolia* 'Hidcote'

NB: For details on a suitable mix for the flowery lawn, please see the box on page 36.

A butterfly mound

Some of the plants most attractive to butterflies grow on chalky soils and are difficult or impossible to grow well if your garden does not happen to be on chalk. In order to overcome this problem we have tried something slightly different with the BTO Nunnery Garden by creating a 'butterfly mound' from a pile of chalk imported to the site. The mound itself is only 4m by 3m (and could in fact be smaller than this) but has proved to be very successful in attracting visiting butterflies and other insects. Although we used chalk you could use rubble as a base. This is typically alkaline in nature.

The chalk and accompanying flint contained a number of larger lumps when it arrived but the chalk has broken down over the last two winters, thanks to the effects of frost. Plants were introduced as plugs, using a selection of suitable species supplied in a peat-free medium. Not all suppliers use a peat-free medium so do ask when selecting plants from a nursery. The plugs were planted straight into the chalk substrate, with no additional soil or fertilizer. These are, after all, plants of poor soils and would soon be out-competed if the fertility were to be increased.

We have found that the different plants have established well, although the Kidney Vetch *Anthyllis vulneraria* did so well that it has had to be hand-weeded from much of the mound in order to prevent it becoming the dominant plant. You may not encounter this particular problem but keep it in mind.

Our choice of species for the mound varies slightly from those listed here (see box, right) because we have, for example, replaced Large Thyme – a thyme able to withstand competition and found across much of southeastern Britain – with Breckland Thyme – an uncommon species found locally to the BTO Nunnery Garden. The Postcode Plants database (http://www.nhm.ac.uk/fff/) proved useful here, though you need to be certain of

Butterfly mound in November 2004 and (below) May 2006 – Mike Toms

the provenance of seed or plants when attempting to use species of a localised distribution. While the chalk may seem like something of a sterile substrate, we have seen the encroachment of grass from the adjoining flowery lawn, something that we have had to manage fairly vigorously.

Plants for a chalk mound

Thrift *Armeria maritima*, Harebell *Campanula rotundifolia*, Large Thyme *Thymus pulegioides*, Wild Thyme *Thymus polystrichus*, Maiden Pink *Dianthus deltoides*, Devil's-bit Scabious *Succisa pratensis*, Common Rock-rose *Helianthemum nummularium*, Kidney Vetch *Anthyllis vulneraria*, Wild Strawberry *Fragaria vesca*, Common Bird's-foot-trefoil *Lotus corniculatus*, Wild Marjoram *Origanum vulgare*, Reflexed Stonecrop *Sedum rupestre*, Biting Stonecrop *Sedum acre*, Daisy *Bellis perennis*, Wild Basil *Clinopodium vulgare*.

Planting scheme for a butterfly mound

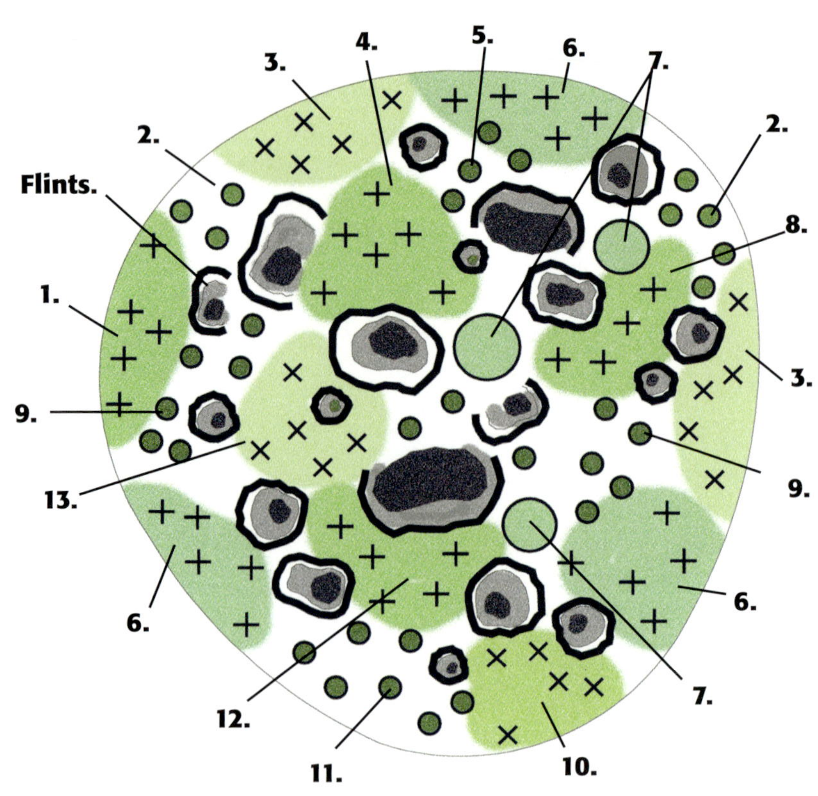

Key to plants used

1. Wild Thyme (*Thymus polytrichus*)
2. Daisy (*Bellis perennis*)
3. Wild Strawberry (*Fragaria vesca*)
4. Common Rock-rose (*Helianthemum nummularium*)
5. Maiden Pink (*Dianthus deltoides*)
6. Creeping thyme (*Thymus serphyllum*)
7. Wild Marjoram (*Origanum vulgare*)
8. Common Bird's-foot-trefoil (*Lotus corniculatus*)
9. Wild Wallflower (*Cheiranthus cheiri*)
10. Biting Stonecrop (*Sedum acre*)
11. Wild Basil (*Clinopodium vulgare*)
12. Harebell (*Campanula rotundifolia*)
13. Thrift (*Armeria maritima*)

Sunny parts of the garden

The more exposed, sunny parts of a garden tend to be fairly easy to deal with because many plants are quite happy with these sorts of conditions. Shade, on the other hand, is often perceived as a problem (see page 46).

Open, south-facing beds are typically dried by the effects of both sun and wind, meaning that the plants lose water through transpiration and need to replenish these losses through the uptake of water from the soil. Since the soils in such situations are often free-draining, the lack of available soil-water may be an issue. This leaves you with two options; the first of which is to plant drought-tolerant species (see page 42) which reduce water loss by means of adaptations to their leaves. The second option is to dig in a quantity of well-rotted organic material. This will improve the water retention of the soil and enable you to grow a wider range of plants.

An additional option is to spread a layer of mulch (ideally of organic material) over the bed, again to reduce water loss (see page 25).

It just so happens that sunny, south-facing beds are attractive to many of the insect species (such as hoverflies, bumblebees and butterflies) that you may wish to encourage in your garden. However, there needs to be some form of shelter from the prevailing wind, since most of these insects will be on the wing. A neighbouring wall, fence or some careful planting of taller shrubs is an ideal solution to this problem, producing exactly the sort of sun-trap that these insects favour.

Creating a sunny bed – As already mentioned, a sunny bed is best positioned in a south-facing location, ideally where it will receive sun through as much of the day as possible. This will allow insects to bask and feed from early morning onwards. Aim to use a range of plant species that offer different foraging opportunities, with a varied array of flowering seasons and flower forms. As you will see elsewhere in this book, such variety is essential when it comes to

Newly-established herbs and shelter – Mike Toms

catering for many of our nectar and pollen feeders. Many of the plants that we regard as herbs are well suited to dry conditions, coming from a Mediterranean climate, and also provide suitable nectaring opportunities for bees and butterflies. As such, they are ideal for planting towards the front of a sunny bed.

Drought-resistant plants – In
addition to the Mediterranean type plants, there are other groups that cope well under dry conditions. Many show similarities in their foliage, sharing features that help to reduce water loss. Drought-resistant plants often have thickened succulent leaves, sometimes waxy in nature, felted or covered in hairs. Sedums, for example, are characterised by their succulent foliage. Other plants have leaves that have been reduced to needles (think of Rosemary). All of these features help to reduce the amount of water lost from the plant through transpiration.

How to use less water – With
increasing demands on our limited water resources we need to reduce the amount that we use on our gardens. The use of drought-resistant plants helps, since such plants need less water, but you can also reduce water use by changing the way in which you manage your borders. In addition to the use of organic material, both in the soil and as a mulch, also

consider establishing a windbreak. Wind increases the rate of transpiration from plant leaves, much in the same way as your washing dries more quickly on a breezy day than on a sunny but still day.

Avoid digging in dry weather, since opening the soil up in this way will increase the rate at which it dries out. Use temporary shade to help new plants establish. We used this approach for the new raised bed in our sunny courtyard garden and it worked extremely well (see photograph). Other options are to avoid frequent light watering, opting instead for a periodic good soaking of those plants that really need the water. This is best carried out in the evening when rates of water loss are lowest. Do try to save and store rainwater in water butts.

Drought-resistant plants

Achillea filipendulina, *Alchemilla mollis*, Betony *Stachys officinalis*, Bloody Crane's-bill *Geranium sanguineum*, Common Evening Primrose *Oenothera biennis*, Common Stork's-bill *Erodium cicutarium* agg., *Dinathus* spp., French Crane's-bill *Geranium endressii*, Garden Cat-mint *Nepeta* x *faassenii*, Globe Thistle *Echinops exaltatus*, Hollyhock *Alcea rosea*, Lavender *Lavandula angustifolia*, Pearly Everlasting *Anaphalis margaritacea*, Pot Marigold *Calendula officinalis*, Red Valerian *Centranthus ruber*, Sea Holly *Eryngium* spp., *Sedum* spp., Snow-in-summer *Cerastium tomentosum*, *Verbascum* spp., Wall Speedwell *Veronica arvensis*, Wild Marjoram *Origanum vulgare*, Yarrow *Achillea millefolium*

Planting scheme for a herb-rich border for insects

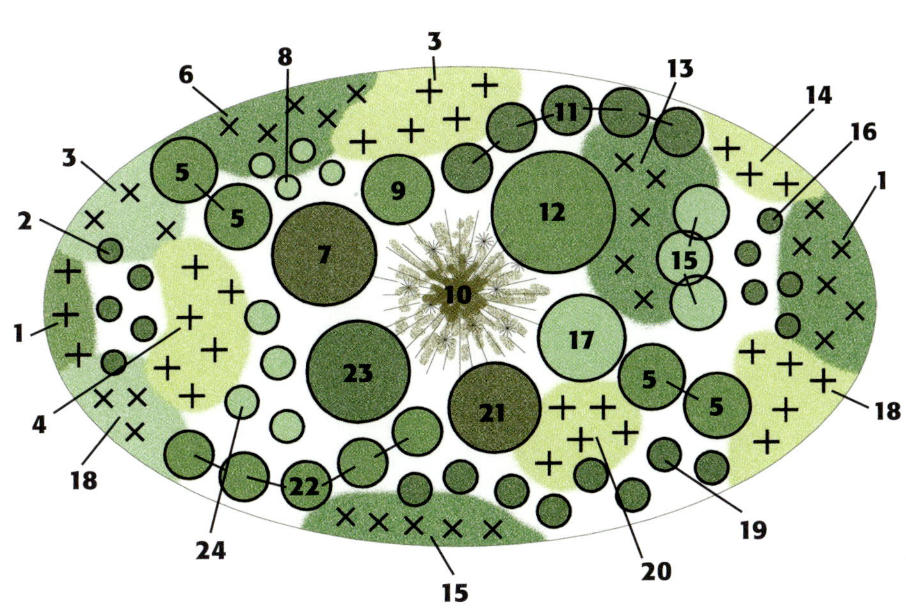

Key to plants used

1. *Thymus serphyllum*
2. *Borago officinalis* (Borage)
3. *Calendula officinalis*
4. *Hypericum perforatum*
5. *Hyssopus officinalis*
6. *Thymus pulegioides*
7. *Salvia officinalis* 'Purpurascens'
8. Anise Hyssop
9. *Tanacetum parthenium* (Feverfew)
10. *Foeniculum vulgare* 'Purpureum' (Bronze Fennel)
11. Lavender 'Hidcote'
12. Rosemary - dwarf
13. *Hesperis matronalis* (Dame's-violet)
14. *Allium schoenoprasum* (Chives)
15. *Oreganum vulgare*
16. *Tanacetum macrophyllum* (Tansy)
17. *Melissa officinalis* (Variegated Lemon Balm)
18. Nasturtium 'Alaska'
19. *Teucrium divaricatum* (Hedge Germander)
20. *Centranthus ruber* (Red Valerian)
21. *Achillea millefolium* (Yarrow)
22. Lavender 'Rosea'
23. Old English lavender
24. *Oreganum vulgare*

Dealing with walls

While the base of a wall can be a difficult position in which to establish a plant, the wall itself can provide support, shelter and raise air temperature in the immediate vicinity (all potentially good for many plants). The soil at the base of a wall is likely to be of poor quality, dry in nature and difficult to work. However, such difficulties are easily overcome, and the use of appropriate shrubs can turn what was a bare wall into an ideal microhabitat for wildlife. The dense evergreen growth of an ivy-covered wall will provide nesting and roosting opportunities for birds, together with shelter and feeding opportunities for a wide range of invertebrates.

While some plants (notably Ivy *Hedera helix* and Canary Island Ivy *Hedera canariensis*) are self-clinging,

Ivy-leaved Toadflax – Mike Toms

others will need support to help them climb the wall. If you are worried about the damage that Ivy might do to your wall, use Canary Island Ivy instead, since this is less prone to rooting into the brickwork. Canary Island Ivy does best in well-drained and alkaline soils, and seems to prefer more sun than our native species. As such you may find that it does better on a south- or east-facing wall than a north-facing one.

There are numerous ways of providing support for climbing plants, from trellis through to wire, and it is simply a matter of choosing which is best for you and the situation in question. Climbers typically require that you improve the soil structure before planting. Do this by digging a hole that is twice the size of the root ball of the plant you are seeking to establish. Fork through the soil in this hole and then add a good quantity of well rotted organic material. Do not plant the climber right up against the wall but, instead, position it 40–50cm away, training it back towards the wall.

Some climbers do best by being pruned and trained to a set form. Others seem to do better if allowed to develop with a rambling habit. Honeysuckle *Lonicera periclymenum*, in particular, does best if allowed to ramble. When selecting climbers, you also need to consider the direction that the wall faces. The conditions can differ markedly depending upon this.

Some plants actually grow on walls, rather than simply climb up them. Ivy-leaved Toadflax *Cymbalaria muralis* is one and, with its delicate pink flowers, it is a great addition to an old flint or stone wall, such as those here at the Nunnery.

Clematis tanguitica – Mike Toms

Planting schemes for walls of different aspects

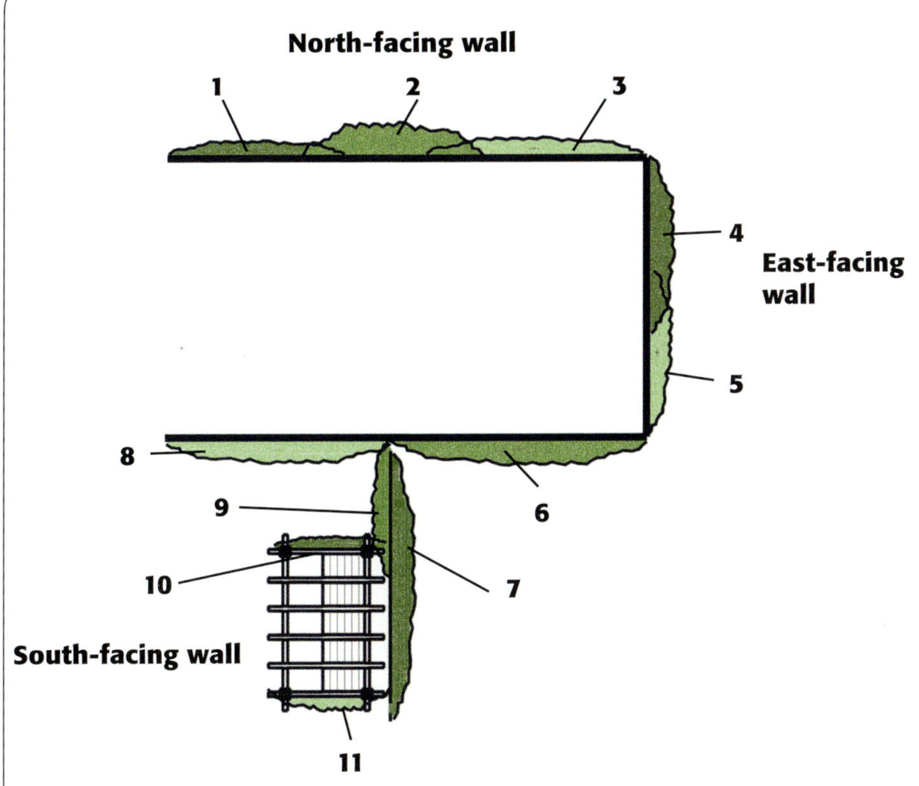

Key to plants used

1. *Hedera helix*
2. *Hydrangea petiolaris*
3. *Pyracantha* spp.
4. *Chaenomeles* spp.
5. *Cotoneaster horizontalis*
6. *Lonicera periclymenum* 'Belgica'
7. *Clematis montana*
8. *Wisteria sinensis*
9. *Jasminum officinale*
10. *Clematis alpina*
11. *Lonicera periclymenum*

Hedera helix – Mike Toms

A shady corner of the BTO Nunnery Garden before planting – Mike Toms

Working with shade

To be honest, shade is not necessarily the problem that many people make it out to be. All you really need to do is choose species that like shade, rather than plant a sun-loving species in shade and then wonder why it does not thrive.

Shade can be subdivided into a number of different forms, from permanent shade (such as under a conifer bush) to partial shade (under the canopy of a thin-crowned, deciduous tree like Silver Birch). Additionally, the soil conditions under an area of shade may be wet or dry and, as a consequence, will favour different plant species.

Some of the shade encountered in gardens will occur under taller deciduous trees and shrubs, producing conditions similar to those seen in many of our broad-leaved woodlands. In such cases, there is typically sufficient light to grow a number of spring-flowering species including Winter Aconite *Eranthis hyemalis*, Wood Anemone *Anemone nemorosa*, Bluebell *Hyacinthoides non-scripta* (make sure you grow the native variety and not the introduced Spanish variety) and Lily-of-the-valley *Convallaria majalis*.

Light levels under this sort of shade are below 50% of those present out in the open. A number of grasses (see box) are able to persist under such conditions but will be lost if light levels

Shade-tolerant plants

Light shade (grasses): Common Bent *Agrostis capillaris*, Crested Dog's-tail *Cynosurus cristatus*, Sweet Vernal Grass *Anthoxanthum odoratum*, Tufted Hair-grass *Deschsampia cespitosa*, Wood Meadow-grass *Poa nemoralis*.

Light shade (flowers): Betony *Stachys officinalis*, Foxglove *Digitalis purpurea*, Garlic Mustard *Alliaria petiolata*, Hedge Bedstraw *Galium mollugo*, Wood Avens *Geum urbanum*, Red Campion *Silene dioica*, Hedge Woundwort *Stachys sylvatica*, Wood Sage *Teucrium scorodonia*, Nettle-leaved Bellflower *Campanula trachelium*, Lungwort *Pulmonaria officinalis*, *Liriope muscari*, Elder *Sambucus nigra*, Perennial Forget-me-not *Brunnera macrophylla*.

Dense shade: Few-flowered Garlic *Allium paradoxum*, Hazelwort *Asarum europaeum*, *Hosta* spp., Ramsons *Allium ursinum*, Three-corned Garlic *Allium triquetrum*, Wood-sorrel *Oxalis acetosella*, Holly *Ilex aquifolium*, Skimmia spp., *Bergenia cordifolia*, *Euonymus fortunei*, Male Fern *Dryopteris flix-mas*, *Mahonia aquifolium*.

Dry shade: Betony *Stachys officinalis*, Perforate St John's-wort *Hypericum perforatum*, Wood Sage *Teucrium scorodonia*, Bugle *Ajuga reptens*, *Geranium macrorrhizum*.

Damp shade: *Astilbe* spp., Greater Periwinkle *Vinca major* 'Variegata', Hedge Woundwort *Stachys sylvatica*, Meadowsweet *Filipendula ulmaria*, Imperforate St John's-wort *Hypericum maculatum*, Pignut *Conopodium majus*, Primrose *Primula vulgaris*, Ragged Robin *Lychnis flos-cuculi*, Royal Fern *Osmunda regalis*, *Hosta* spp., *Helleborus* spp., Soft Shield Fern *Polystichum setiferum*.

Planting scheme for a shady corner

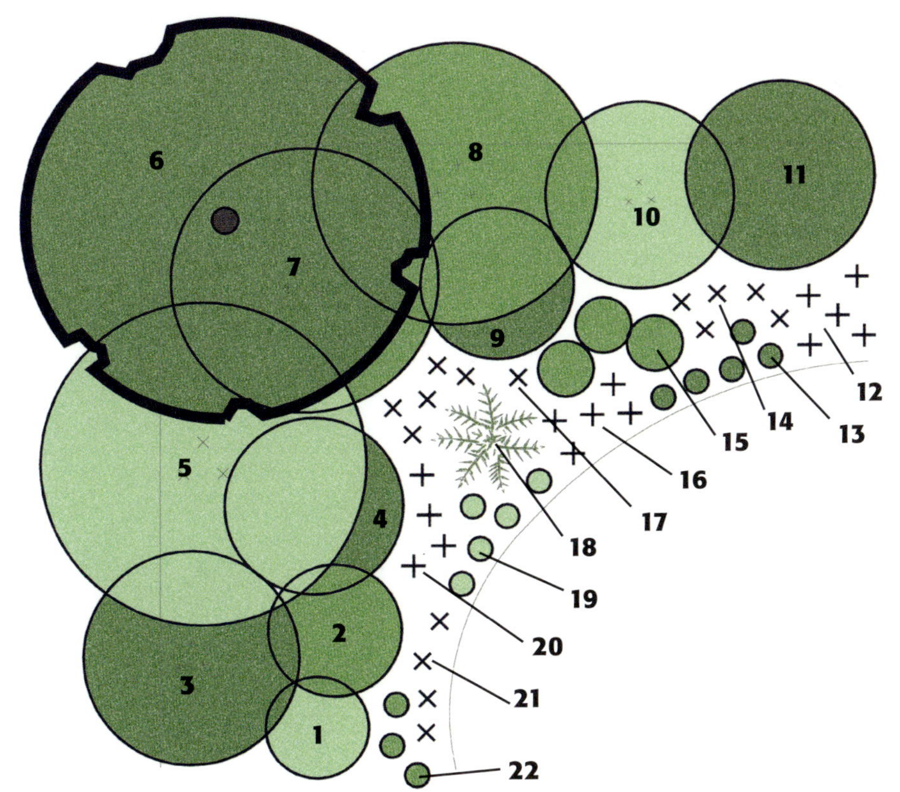

Key to plants used

1. *Hypericum* 'Hidcote'
2. *Viburnum opulus* 'Compactum'
3. *Ilex aquifolium* 'Argentea Marginata'
4. *Cotoneaster franchetii*
5. *Sambucus nigra* 'Black Beauty'
6. *Sorbus aucuparia*
7. *Viburnum tinus* 'Eve Price'
8. *Amelanchier lamarkii*
9. *Mahonia aquifolium*
10. *Euonymus europaeus* 'Red Cascade'
11. *Rhamnus alaterna* 'Argenteovariegata'
12. *Pulmonaria* 'Sissinghurst White'
13. *Primula vulgaris*
14. *Silene dioica*
15. *Euphorbia amygdaloides purpurea*
16. *Ajuga reptans*
17. *Digitalis purpurea*
18. *Polystichum setiferum*
19. *Lamium galeobdolon* 'Hermann's Pride'
20. *Campanula latifolia*
21. *Geranium macrorrhizum* 'Album'
22. *Lunaria annua*

drop to below 25% of those seen in the open. Under these circumstances you are limited to flowers but if you are looking for ground cover then consider Great Periwinkle *Vinca major*.

Courtyard gardens

There may be instances where you do not have the option of being able to dig down into the ground to create a flowerbed. This sort of circumstance is most often encountered in small urban courtyard gardens, which may also be shaded by buildings or trees.

One solution is to use raised beds and pots to create your garden. Given a sufficiently large pot or raised bed it is even possible to grow small shrubs, such as the North American blueberry *Vaccinium corymbosum* or dwarf varieties of fruit trees (try the crab apple John Downie on a dwarfing rootstock).

Many plants will grow quite happily in anything from an old bucket through to a smart terracotta pot. Just make sure that it is sturdy enough when filled with a peat-free potting compost, has suitable drainage holes and (ideally) is frost-proof. Because containers tend to dry out quite quickly, try to use ones that are as deep as possible. Containers planted with large plants should be anchored to prevent them from blowing over in the wind.

Raised beds can be made from a range of materials, including bricks, railway sleepers or recycled materials. We have used locally-sourced oak timbers, cut to size, which should last for at least 20 years. Try to avoid using softwoods, like pine, which have a very limited durability (lasting for about five years). One of the beauties of using a timber like oak is that it does not need to be treated, thus avoiding the need to use any chemical wood preservatives. Pressure-treated timber is best avoided as it will have been chemically-treated.

The small amount of space available in many urban gardens is not necessarily an issue since you can come up with a planting plan that fits the space. Avoid using plants that are too big for the garden as they may make it look unbalanced but do try to use some evergreen cover, highly favoured by visiting House Sparrows. Our suggested planting plan combines a number of different elements, including early season nectar (*Pulmonaria* spp.), cover and berries for visiting birds (*Hedera* spp.).

Newly planted raised bed to prevent damage to hidden archaeology – Mike Toms

A courtyard garden with raised beds and pots

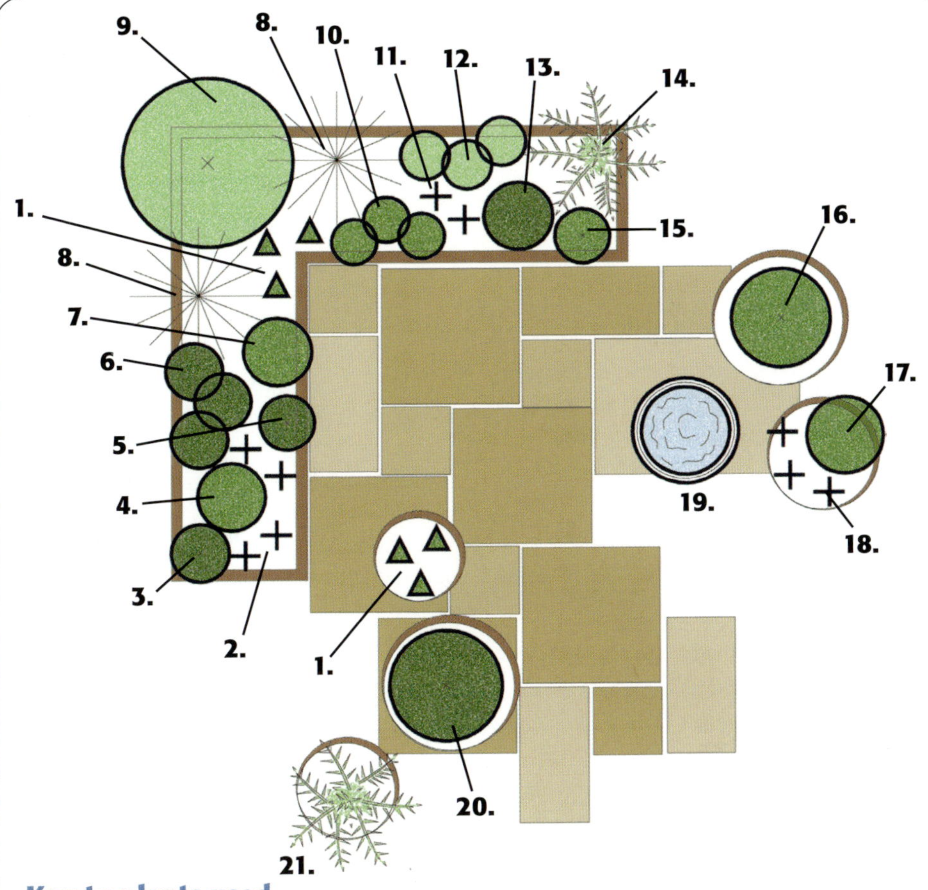

Key to plants used

1. *Viola tricolor* x 6
2. *Ajuga reptans* x 4
3. *Hedera helix*
4. *Geranium phaeum* 'Album'
5. *Pulmonaria longifolia*
6. *Digitalis purpurea* x 3
7. *Alchemilla mollis*
8. *Carex buchananii* x 2
9. *Skimmia japonica* 'Veitchii'
10. *Lamium maculatum* 'Beacon Silver' x 3
11. *Aquilegia vulgaris* x 2
12. *Campanula glomerata* ' Superba' x 3
13. *Euphorbia amygdaloides* 'Purpurea'
14. *Polystichum setiferum*
15. *Liriope muscari*
16. *Daphne odora* 'Aureomarginata'
17. *Helleborus orientalis*
18. *Narcissus* 'Jet Fire' x 3
19. Bird bath
20. *Vaccinium corymbosum*
21. *Asplenium scolopendrium*

No matter how small your patch, there is always space to include an area that is either deliberately left unmanaged or is managed in such a way that it comes to resemble a more natural habitat. This could be something as simple as a woodpile tucked behind taller shrubs or a tiny pond just a few feet across. Alternatively, if you have the space, then there is scope to create something far grander, like a wildflower meadow – you could even make this the centrepiece of your garden! This section of the book deals with two main topics, the establishment of meadows and the creation of ponds. Both can make a big difference to the wildlife value of a garden, even if created on a small scale. While a small pond may not support the range of species that a larger version could, it should still attract wildlife that would not be able to use your garden were these features not present.

Meadows & mini-meadows

There is something special about a meadow at the height of summer; the buzzing of grasshoppers and bees, the scent of flowers and the sight of many different plants competing for space. While a true meadow (one that has developed through decades of favourable management) may support hundreds of species, it is still possible to create a cut-down version in your garden; a version that still offers great wildlife benefits. In fact you do not need a large area in which to establish a meadow (even though bigger does tend to be better). It could be a strip alongside an existing lawn or a small corner of the garden tucked away from the house (both of which can be thought of as 'mini-meadows'). Alternatively, if you want something that retains a degree of formality, go instead for a flowery lawn (see page 36).

Meadow basics – Start by looking at your garden and thinking about what sort of meadow you want and where it should be placed. The important things to consider are soil type, soil pH, drainage, shade and when you want it to flower. These factors will determine the range of plant species that you can grow (see page 53 for recommendations) and, in turn, the type of meadow you will end up with. The flowering times of the plants within the meadow will determine when the meadow should be cut (see page 52). You also need to decide whether to plant into an existing grassy sward or start from scratch by seeding onto bare soil.

Bee-fly *Bombylius major* – Mike Toms

Planting into an existing sward

– Although simply scattering seeds over an existing sward will not bring success (the seeds will not be able to compete with the already-established grasses), it is possible to get a meadow going by either removing squares of turf within the sward, and then seeding them, or by adding established plug plants to the sward. Yellow Rattle *Rhinanthus minor* is particularly useful in this context because it is a root-hemiparasite of various grasses (and more competitive plant species) and reduces their competitive vigour. Plug plants are best added to a sward during autumn or spring when the other plants are short and less competitive.

Starting from scratch

– Since an existing sward will typically have a highly fertile soil and be dominated by established grasses, it can be very difficult to establish those meadow plants that favour soils of low fertility. Because of this, starting from scratch with bare soil and a seed mix is really the best way to establish a meadow. Assuming that you are starting from scratch and have removed the turf, the next stage is to lower the soil fertility. This can be done in several ways; either by i) removing the top 20-30cm of fertile soil, ii) turning over the soil to bring the less fertile sub-soil to the surface or iii) growing a nutrient 'hungry' crop (like potatoes) in the preceding season (the least efficient option). The meadow at the BTO Nunnery Gardens was created by turning the soil over to bring sub-soil to the surface, a method that appears to have worked well.

Once you have lowered the fertility you are ready to prepare the seed bed by raking and then lightly rolling or trampling the surface. You may need to deal with any weed seeds. Determine which plants you wish to establish and then source the seed from a reputable supplier (see box). Try to select species that are known to grow locally and, if possible, try and source seed of local provenance (since this helps to maintain the genetic heritage of plants). In addition to straight batches of individual species, specialist suppliers offer a range of seed mixes, each designed for particular conditions or meadow types. The mix should include both wildflowers (20%) and grasses (80%), since the resulting meadow should, by definition, be a mixture of both. Work on the assumption that you will need sufficient seed to achieve a sowing rate of some 3-4g/m^2, though seek advice from the supplier for your particular choice. This rate is roughly 10% of that used for a formal lawn.

It is best to sow the seeds in early autumn since the seeds of some species (*e.g.* crane's-bills and Cowslip) require a cold spell to break their dormancy. However, you can sow in March or April and accept that some of the seeds won't germinate until the following year. You may find that you can achieve a more even spread of seed by mixing it with damp silver sand, before broadcasting it by hand across the prepared seedbed.

Sourcing seed

Wildflower seed mixes are available from many different suppliers. However, the provenance of the seed is not always clear and it is best to avoid purchasing seed of unknown origin. Because individual plant species may show significant regional variation in their genetic make-up, locally harvested seed is best. The commercial availability of such seed is limited at present but improving all the time, so do ensure that you purchase seed that is, at least, of British origin. The seed used in the BTO Nunnery Gardens was supplied by Emorsgate Seeds (see Resources, page 91).

The first shoots should appear the following spring and the meadow will continue to develop slowly over the next few years (it may appear sparse at first but do not let this worry you). Like us, you may find that some species establish themselves quickly and become an important part of the community during the first few years, gradually dropping out and becoming less important as other species establish. The BTO meadow was initially dominated by Corn Chamomile *Anthemis arvensis* (part of a cornfield nurse (see below) which has now virtually disappeared.

Cornfield Nurse – Adding cornfield annuals to the mixture as a first year 'nurse crop' is a marvellous way to start off a meadow. This gives a colourful display in the first summer and helps to protect the young meadow plants. The cornfield annuals suppress weeds and hold back early growth of the faster growing grasses and flowering perennials. This leads to a more open and diverse meadow sward. It is, however, important to cut back the cornfield annuals as soon as flowering is over, as they can then inhibit the young meadow plants growing beneath. As usual all cuttings must be removed.

Cutting regimes

Spring meadow: Flowers from March to late June or early July. Cut in mid-July and allow hay to dry *in situ* before removal from the site. Take occasional cuts from July through into October. Suitable species to establish include: Cowslip, Cuckooflower, Meadow Buttercup, Salad Burnet, Common Sorrel, Red Campion Selfheal and Snakeshead Fritillary.

Summer meadow: Flowers from July through into September. Make occasional cuts in March and April if wanted and then allow to grow up and flower from early May all the way through to late August. Take a hay cut in August or September and remove the clippings. Species to establish include: Bladder Campion, Common Knapweed, Field Scabious, Meadow Cranesbill, Oxeye Daisy, Ragged Robin, Selfheal and Yellow Rattle.

Aftercare – Unless using a cornfield nurse, the meadow should be cut (in its first year) once it reaches about 10cm in height to keep the grasses under control. This is not essential though, and can be left if you are happy for things to develop more slowly. However, if you have included a cornfield mix or Yellow Rattle then you should never cut the meadow in its first year. If you do cut, then maintain a regime that fits the meadow type (see box above). A spring-flowering meadow should be cut in mid-July (*i.e.* after the flowers have shed their seed) and then cut as necessary throughout the late summer and autumn. A summer flowering meadow is not normally cut until early May and is then left uncut agin until late September or October. Remember to remove the clippings to keep the fertility levels within the soil down, thus favouring less competitive species. Also maintain some areas of bare ground and control the build-up of thatch.

Cornflower – Mike Toms

The following list gives a range of plants which can be used to create meadows under different conditions. The list shows species suitable for chalky, sandy or wet soils, together with those suited to a meadow mix with a high grass content. * grasses

Species	Latin	Chalky	Sandy	Wet	Grassy
Agrimony	Agrimonia eupatoria	-	-	-	G
Bird's-foot-trefoil	Lotus corniculatus	C	-	-	-
Bulbous Buttercup	Ranunculus bulbosus	-	S	-	-
Cock's-foot*	Dactylis glomerata	-	-	-	G
Common Knapweed	Centaurea nigra	-	S	W	-
Common Vetch	Vicia sativa	-	-	-	G
Cowslip	Primula veris	C	-	W	-
Crested Dog's-tail*	Cynosurus cristatus	C	S	W	G
Devil's-bit Scabious	Succisa pratensis	-	-	W	-
Field Scabious	Knautia arvensis	C	-	-	-
Great Burnet	Sanguisorba officinalis	-	-	W	-
Greater Knapweed	Centaurea scabiosa	C	-	-	-
Hedge Bedstraw	Galium mollugo	-	-	-	G
Hoary Plantain	Plantago media	C	-	-	-
Kidney Vetch	Anthyllis vulneraria	C	-	-	-
Lady's Bedstraw	Galium verum	C	S	W	-
Meadow Fescue*	Festuca pratensis	-	-	-	G
Meadow Buttercup	Ranunculus acris	C	S	W	-
Meadow Foxtail*	Alopecurus pratensis	-	-	W	-
Meadowsweet	Filipendula ulmaria	-	-	W	-
Meadow Vetchling	Lathyrus pratensis	-	-	-	G
Musk Mallow	Malva moschata	-	S	-	-
Oxeye Daisy	Leucanthemum vulgare	C	S	W	-
St John's-wort	Hypericum perforatum	-	-	-	G
Quaking Grass*	Briza media	C	-	-	-
Ragged Robin	Lychnis flos-cuculi	-	-	W	-
Red Campion	Silene dioica	-	-	-	G
Ribwort Plantain	Plantago lanceolata	-	S	-	-
Rough Hawkbit	Leontodon hispidus	C	-	-	-
Salad Burnet	Sanguisorba minor	C	-	-	-
Sheep's-fescue*	Festuca ovina	C	S	-	-
Sweet Vernal Grass*	Anthoxanthum odoratum	-	S	-	-
Tall Fescue*	Festuca arundinacea	-	-	-	G
Tufted Vetch	Vicia cracca	-	-	-	G
Upright Hedge Parsley	Torilis japonica	-	-	-	G
Viper's-bugloss	Echium vulgare	-	S	-	-
Wild Carrot	Daucus carota	C	-	-	G
Yarrow	Achillea millefolium	C	S	W	-

The water of life

Water brings a garden to life, instantly increasing its attractiveness to wildlife. It can also provide a strong focus, adding a different dimension to the garden and, if moving water is present, a new sound. Water is usually present either as a garden pond or in the form of a bird bath. This section examines how the first of these two features can be incorporated into a garden and looks at what can be achieved with relatively little effort.

Garden ponds

A typical garden pond will support a diverse ecosystem, most of which will have arrived under its own steam. Some of the animals which benefit from the presence of a pond spend their lives within its watery confines, others use it on a more casual basis. Common Frogs may use the pond for spawning, while various hoverflies, craneflies and other insects may also have an aquatic phase. Larger creatures (like birds, mammals and Grass Snakes) may visit the pond to drink or feed. In fact, the range of creatures that will use your pond is really rather

Smooth Newt – Mike Toms

staggering. A number of different factors will determine how attractive a pond is for wildlife. These include pond shape, position, age, depth and how it is planted. Based on the research that has been carried out over the last 30 years we can make recommendations about the effects of such factors on the value of a pond.

Position – Since water temperature has a strong influence on pond life, a new pond is best sited away from excessive shade but not necessarily right out in the open, separated from other, cover-providing, features. An open aspect, but with good surrounding vegetation is ideal. High temperatures during the establishment phase may promote the unwanted growth of filamentous algae.

Size – Although there are some species that prefer larger ponds, small ponds are usually just as valuable as larger ones. However, depth is important in order to provide an ice-free refuge during the worst of the winter weather. A depth of 70–80cm is ideal for the middle of a pond, surrounded by sloping shallows.

Shape – A pond that is irregular in shape will have more edge and will offer a range of different microclimates. It will also tend to look more natural, which is a good thing from a design point of view.

Vegetation – Submerged plants oxygenate the water, provide cover from predators and offer places for aquatic

Starling – Jill Pakenham

invertebrates to deposit their eggs. Ponds with lots of submerged plants support more creatures than those without. Marginal vegetation is also important, again supporting a range of creatures but also softening the transition from one habitat feature into another.

Fish – The widely held view that a pond with fish is very poor for wildlife is not entirely supported by published research. However, in general, ponds with fish support a reduced community of species and tend to be very similar in the sorts of species that they do support. Ponds without fish have more individuals of more species and show greater variation from one pond to another.

Constructing a pond

Before you start digging, you need to think about how you want the pond to look and where it will be positioned. Then you need to decide upon the material from which the pond will be constructed. Pre-formed pond shells can be purchased from most garden centres but we would recommend using a flexible liner, either of top-quality PVC or butyl rubber. These are tough and allow you to create a pond that will best fit your garden and what you hope to achieve. The following guidelines for constructing a pond therefore assume that you are using a flexible liner.

Start by marking out the shape of the pond with pegs, and also consider using a similar approach for the shelves of

varying depth that will be created within the pond itself. Use a spirit or laser level to make sure that the top of the pond is level. Next, calculate the amount of pond liner that you need. The length required is equivalent to the length of the pond plus twice the maximum depth and the width is calculated in the same way.

We would recommend using a system of layers when installing the liners, in order to produce a natural look and prevent leaks. First a 5cm layer of sand isolates the liner from any sharp stones beneath. The liner itself is then sandwiched between two layers of protective 'pond underlay'. This is a geotextile available from suppliers of pond liners. Old carpet is best avoided as this rots away over time. Use of a top layer of fabric (see photo) allows the pond to be back filled with 7cm of subsoil. This will give the pond a natural appearance.

The link between the soil in the pond and that outside also creates a moist margin around the pond which can be planted with marginals like Ragged Robin and Cuckooflower. During the establishment phase there may be some wicking, with water evaporating from this damp marginal soil. However, this ceases to be a problem once the plants become established. Begin filling the pond with water once you have back filled with soil almost up to the edges. Rainwater is best, although tap water is fine; a water butt is one means by which the pond can be filled. Once the pond is nearly full, and the liner has settled with the weight of water, the edges can be buried. Allow the pond to settle for a couple of days before you begin planting.

Planting your pond – A good pond will contain a mixture of oxygenators, open water plants and marginals. We would recommend using native plants for your pond but there are some good non-natives. There are definitely some plants which should be avoided, notably New Zealand Pigmyweed *Crassula helmsii*, Nutall's Waterweed *Elodea nuttallii*, Water Fern *Azolla filiculoides*, Parrot's Feather *Myriophyllum aquaticum* and Floating Pennywort *Hydroctyle ranunculoides*. Plants can be bought from garden or aquatic suppliers. Plant straight into the soil, supporting plants with stones where necessary. To create a natural effect, try to plant in drifts – placing a few single plants among groups of others. Different species will have different needs, especially planting depths, and it is important to bear this in mind when selecting plants and in deciding where to put them (see box). Lilies are best planted in baskets so that they can be easily thinned.

Care of your pond – Just like any other aspect of your garden, you will need to manage your pond, by thinning out plants as things develop and by keeping an eye on water and nutrient levels. In particular, watch out for the build up of green filamentous algae, which can

OPEN WATER PLANTS

Amphibious Bistort *Persicaria amphibia*, Fringed Water-lily *Nymphoides peltata*, Frogbit *Hydrocharis morsus-ranae*, Yellow Water-lily *Nuphar lutea*, Water-soldier *Stratiotes aloides*, White Water-lily *Nymphaea alba*, Common Water-crowfoot *Ranunculus aquatilis* and Water-violet *Hottonia palustris*.

Yellow Iris – Dawn Balmer

PLANTS FOR DAMP EDGES

Meadowsweet *Filipendula ulmaria*, Marsh Woundwort *Stachys palustris*, Water Avens *Geum rivale*, Ragged Robin *Lychnis flos-cuculi*, Greater Bird's-foot-trefoil *Lotus pedunculatus*, Red Campion *Silene dioica*, Bugle *Ajuga reptans*, Cuckooflower *Cardamine pratensis*, Hemp-agrimony *Eupatorium cannabinum*, Primrose *Primula vulgaris* and Meadow Vetchling *Lathyrus pratensis*.

Fringed Lily – Mike Toms

OXYGENATORS

Curled Pondweed *Potamogeton crispus*[1], Common Water-starwort *Callitriche stagnalis*, Rigid Hornwort *Ceratophyllum demersum* and Spiked Water Milfoil *Myriophyllum spicatum*.

[1] NB: can be difficult to control

MARGINALS

Arrowhead *Sagittaria sagittifolia*, Bogbean *Menyanthes trifoliata*, Brooklime *Veronica beccabunga*, Yellow Iris *Iris pseudacorus*, Marsh-marigold *Caltha palustris*, Hard Rush *Juncus inflexus*, Cyperus Sedge *Cyperus pseudocyperus*, Remote Sedge *Carex remota*, Lesser Spearwort *Ranunculus flammula*, Water Forget-me-not *Myosotis scorpioides*, Water-plantain *Alisma plantago-aquatica*, Blue Water-speedwell *Veronica anagallis-aquatica*, Water-cress *Rorippa nasturtium-aquaticum* and Purple Loosestrife *Lythrum salicaria*.

CROSS SECTION THROUGH A POND

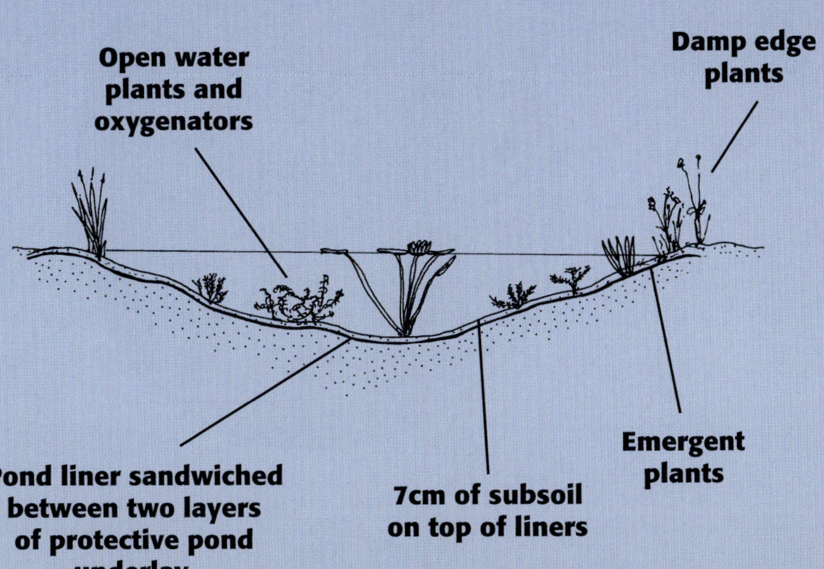

Planting scheme for a garden pond

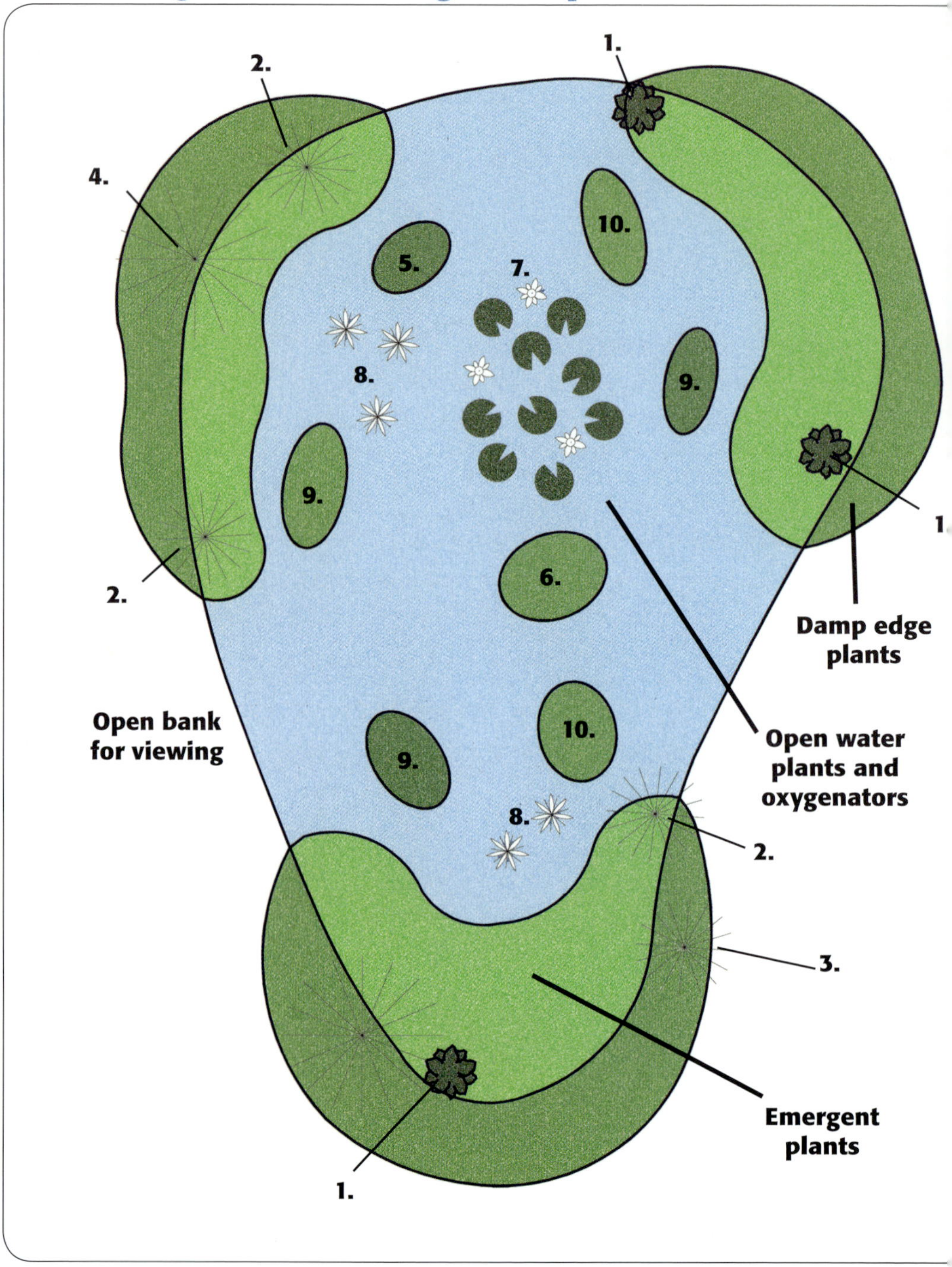

Emergent plants

Arrowhead *Saggitaria sagittifolia*
Bogbean *Menyanthes trifoliata*
Flowering Rush *Butomus umbellatus*
Yellow Iris *Iris pseudacorus*
Purple Loosestrife *Lythrum salicaria*
Marsh Marigold *Caltha palustris* **(1.)**
Lesser Reedmace *Typha angustifolia*
Soft Rush *Juncus efusus* **(2.)**
Cyperus Sedge *Carex pseudocyperus*
Lesser Spearwort *Ranunculus flammula*
Water Forget-me-not *Myosotis scorpiodes*
Water Mint *Mentha aquatica*
Water Plantain *Alisma plantago aquatica*
Water Speedwell *Veronica anagallis-aquatica*

Damp edge plants

Brooklime *Veronica beccabunga*
Bugle *Ajuga reptans*
Meadow Buttercup *Ranunculus acris*
Red Campion *Silene dioica*
Lesser Celandine *Ranunculus ficaria*
Cuckooflower *Cardamine pratensis*
Hemp Agrimony *Eupatorium cannabinum*
Meadowsweet *Filipendula ulmaria*
Primrose *Primula vulgaris*
Ragged Robin *Lychnis flos-cuculi*
Hard Rush *Juncus inflexus* **(3.)**
Soft Rush *Juncus efusus* **(2.)**
Devil's-bit Scabious *Succisa pratensis*
Cyperus Sedge *Carex pseudocyperus*
Pendulous Sedge *Carex pendula* **(4.)**
Remote Sedge *Carex remota*
Selfheal *Prunella vulgaris*
Meadow Vetchling *Lathyrus pratensis*
Water Avens *Geum rivale*
Water Mint *Mentha aquatica*
March Woundwort *Stachys palustris*

Open water plants and oxygenators

Amphibious Bistort *Persicaria amphibium* **(5.)**
Rigid Hornwort *Ceratophyllum demersum*
Common Water-starwort *Callitriche stagnalis* **(9.)**
Curled Pondweed *Potamogeton crispus*
Spiked-water Milfoil *Myriophyllum spicatum*
Water Hawthorn *Aponogeton distachyos* **(6.)**
White Water Lily *Nymphaea alba* **(7.)**
Water Soldier *Stratiotes aloides* **(8.)**
Water-violet *Hottonia palustris* **(10.)**

If you don't mind eventual total surface cover then add Fringed Water Lily *Nymphoides peltata* and/ or Broad-leaved Pond Weed *Potamogeton natans*.

sometimes be treated with barley straw. Blanket weed is a pioneer species which will take advantage of the open spaces and nutrients in the water of a new pond. Remove it regularly by twining it around a cane and it will decline as other pond plants establish themselves and shade it out. Place any weed that you remove by the side of the pond so that aquatic creatures can find their way back into the water. As the pond matures you will also need to thin out some of the other plants. Those planted in baskets within the pond should be lifted and thinned every three years or so to keep them under control. If you do not do this, they will spread from the baskets and invade the mud at the bottom of the pond. Thinning can be carried out as a regular and small-scale process. Alternatively, you can give the pond a good autumn clearout but do avoid doing this in spring or early summer when much of the pond's wildlife will be breeding.

Small pools for wildlife –

Because water is such an important feature within any wildlife garden, it should be provided even if you do not have the space for a fully-blown pond! Wildlife can even be attracted to a pool created using an up-turned dustbin lid. Small pools, such as this, are prone to drying out and there is also the risk that the quality of the water will deteriorate. However, if carefully planned, then it is possible to create a small pool in a shady position that is just a couple of feet across and self-sustaining. Because of its shallow nature, such a pond may well freeze solid during the winter – something that is likely to create a temporary and highly seasonal pond fauna.

Of course, small ponds are not just inhabited by animals and plants, they are also used by other species for drinking and bathing. If landscaped into their surroundings (as is the case with the small pool shown below) they should pull in a range of different bird and mammal species.

Whitethroat visiting a small pool, made from an upturned dustbin lid – Jill Pakenham

PLANTS FOR BIRDS

While some shrubs and trees provide nesting opportunities (cavities or thick cover), others offer feeding opportunities (berries, seeds and invertebrates). As we have already seen, the types and species of flowers, shrubs and trees that you choose to establish within your garden will have an influence on which bird species visit. This influence may be direct, through the provision of suitable berry-producing shrubs, or it may be indirect, by using plants that attract insects, which in turn attract insectivorous birds.

This section of the book looks in greater detail at the relationships between plants, insects and birds, drawing upon the scientific literature to produce lists of plant species that are valuable for particular roles. Starting with plants that provide shelter and nesting cover, we then move on to look at plants providing fruits and seeds, before turning our attention to those which support particular groups of invertebrates.

Nesting and roosting cover

Research suggests that it is the presence of feeding opportunities that largely determines which tree and shrub species are most attractive to birds. Feeding insectivorous birds, for example, have been shown to prefer feeding in Sycamore as opposed

Birch – Mike Toms

to Beech, the former presumably supporting a greater biomass of the invertebrates preferred by the bird species under study (see box on page 63). However, access to nesting sites may also be important and we might expect to see a preference for those tree and shrub species providing suitable nesting opportunities.

We know that different trees and shrubs vary greatly in terms of the availability of cavities, foliage density and limb architecture. Since the requirements of the different bird species also vary, we should expect to see a pattern of association emerge. For example, within mixed-conifer plantations, foliage-nesting songbirds show a clear preference for nesting in spruces, selecting them over opportunities on offer in pines, firs and Larch. It seems likely that this preference is linked to the greater foliage density found in spruce (*i.e.* more cover around the nest). The degree of association is likely to be stronger for those species which have specialist requirements, than for those with a more generalist approach.

The nest site requirements of most of our woodland birds have been well-studied and it is possible to draw conclusions about some of the associations shown with particular tree species. However, most gardens lack the range of nesting opportunities on offer in a typical broadleaved or coniferous woodland. For one thing, there tends to be very little in the way of standing dead wood available in gardens. This greatly restricts the natural nesting opportunities available to cavity nesters, though the provision of suitable nestboxes can counter this for some, though not all, species (see page 82 for more on the provision of nestboxes).

Goldcrest – John Harding

Trees for wildlife

An examination of published research demonstrates that most tree species are of significant value to wildlife, regardless of whether or not they are native in origin. However, certain tree species are clearly better for particular organisms and, as a general rule, the length of time that a tree species has been present in Britain, together with its abundance, shows a positive association with its use (as measured by species richness). Even the much-maligned Sycamore *Acer pseudoplatanus* has value. It flowers in high summer (when few other trees are flowering), supports a large biomass of foliage-feeding invertebrates (great for insectivorous birds) and its initially smooth bark supports a number of nationally rare epiphytes. Trees also support communities associated with dead wood and leaf litter, together with soil-living fungi and the organisms that feed on them. Many of these are easily overlooked, thus lowering the importance of the tree in our eyes. Fortunately, an attempt has been made to qualify and (to an extent) quantify the value of widespread trees and shrubs. This work, carried out by Keith Alexander, Jill Butler and Ted Green (see Resources Section), is summarised in the following table.

Tree species (score out of 45)	Particularly good for
Oak (natives) *Quercus* spp. (39)	Fungi, wood-decay and foliage invertebrates, fruits/seeds, epiphytes
Birches *Betula* spp. (34)	Fungi, wood-decay and foliage invertebrates, fruits/seeds, epiphytes
Sycamore *Acer pseudoplatanus* (31)	Foliage invertebrates, leaf litter, pollen/nectar, epiphytes
Beech *Fagus sylvatica* (31)	Fungi, wood-decay invertebrates, fruits/seeds, epiphytes
Goat Willow *Salix caprea* (30)	Foliage invertebrates, pollen/nectar, epiphytes
Hawthorn *Crataegus monogyna* (30)	Foliage invertebrates, leaf litter, pollen/nectar, fruits/seeds
Scots Pine *Pinus sylvestris* (27)	Fungi, wood-decay and foliage invertebrates, fruits/seeds
Ash *Fraxinus excelsior* (27)	Wood-decay invertebrates, leaf litter, epiphytes
Hazel *Corylus avellana* (26)	Leaf litter, epiphytes
Limes *Tilia* spp. (25)	Fungi, leaf litter, pollen/nectar
Alder *Alnus glutinosa* (23)	Foliage invertebrates, fruits/seeds
Rowan *Sorbus aucuparia* (23)	Leaf litter, pollen/nectar, fruits/seeds
Poplars *Populus* spp. (22)	Foliage invertebrates
Field Maple *Acer campestre* (21)	Pollen/nectar
Holly *Ilex aquifolium* (20)	Pollen/nectar, fruits/seeds
European Larch *Larix decidua* (20)	Fungi, fruits/seeds
Hornbeam *Carpinus betulus* (19)	–
Horse Chestnut *Aesculus hippocastanum* (18)	Pollen/nectar
Yew *Taxus baccata* (16)	Fruits/seeds
London Plane *Platanus* x *hispanica* (7)	–

Adapted from Alexander *et al.* 2006. *British Wildlife* 18 (1), 18-28

Pyracantha – Mike Toms

A number of the bird species to use gardens for breeding will make their first nesting attempt of the year in an evergreen shrub. Such shrubs provide good cover at a time when most broad-leaved trees are still in bud. This means that a range of ornamental conifers and evergreen shrubs should be considered when thinking about the provision of nesting opportunities within your garden. Although some of these may be native (*e.g.* Holly and Yew) you may find that introduced conifers provide you with cover more quickly, typically being faster growing.

Several ornamental varieties of *Chamaecyparis* (cypresses) are ideal for this purpose. Recommended varieties (typically showing a narrow conical habit) are *Chamaecyparis lawsoniana* 'Ellwoodii' (grows to 10ft), *Chamaecyparis lawsoniana* 'Minima' (grows to 5ft and is more rounded in shape), and *Chamaecyparis lawsoniana* 'Gnome' (also rounded, growing to just 3ft). The shorter varieties will be used by Dunnock, the taller additionally by Greenfinch and Goldfinch. If you want a bit of instant height but not too much width (c. 4ft), then *Chamaecyparis lawsoniana* 'Columnaris' should reach 30ft fairly quickly, providing both nesting opportunities and a suitable song perch.

Other evergreen options include Holly *Ilex aquifolium* (which will also provide berries and flowers, assuming that you have both male and female plants present) and Yew *Taxus baccata* (though note that this species is toxic to mammals). *Cotoneaster franchetti*, *Pyracantha atalantiodes* and Ivy *Hedera helix*, can be particularly useful for evergreen nesting and roosting cover; all also producing berries. Another climber worth considering for evergreen nesting

cover is honeysuckle, not the native species *Lonicera periclymenum*, which (although great for berries and nesting cover later in the year) is not evergreen, but *Lonicera henryi* – an evergreen species from China which is semi-hardy and produces black berries.

Deciduous species come into their own later in the breeding season and many species have a structure that provides nesting opportunities. Various finches will make use of shrubs and small trees, including fruit trees, choosing to nest in the fork of a branch or up against the trunk, while others will utilise the cover afforded by a native hedge. Some species will nest low down in scruffy vegetation, such as Bramble *Rubus fruticosus* agg. (Blackbird, Robin, Blackcap) or a nettle bed (Whitethroat).

Some of the best shrubs are those which produce thick, thorny cover; the thorns adding an extra level of deterrent to potential nest predators. Hawthorn *Crataegus monogyna* is particularly

Trees/shrubs for shelter and nesting cover

Berberis darwinii, *Berberis gagnepainii*, Blackthorn *Prunus spinosa*, Box *Buxus sempervirens*,  *Cotoneaster lacteus*, *Cotoneaster horizontalis*, *Elaegnus ebbingei*, Hawthorn *Crataegus monogyna*, Holly *Ilex aquifolium*, Ivy *Hedera helix*, *Laurus nobilis*, Lawson Cypress *Chamaecyparis lawsoniana*, Leyland Cypress x *Cupressocyparis leylandii*, *Lonicera henryi*, Privet *Ligustrum vulgare*, *Prunus laurocerastus*, *Prunus lusitanica*, *Pyracantha* spp., Sea-buckthorn *Hippophae rhamnoides*, *Viburnum fragrans*, *Viburnum tinus*, Yew *Taxus baccata*.

good in this respect, as are many of the different *Berberis* and *Pyracanytha* species; select a variety that is best suited to the location in which you wish to establish it.

In coastal gardens, Sea-buckthorn *Hippophae rhamnoides* can be particularly useful. Tolerant of the salty conditions, it provides shelter, nesting opportunities and berries (although, since it is dioecious you will need both female and male plants – present in a ratio of 3:1 – to get berries). Other useful plants for a coastal garden are *Cotoneaster lacteus*, *Euonymus japonicus* and *Viburnum tinus*.

Although many suitable shrubs can be established as 'stand-alone' bushes, others may be better placed alongside a wall (see page 44) or as part of a hedge. These two approaches are particularly good if you only have a small garden, since the chances are that you will have a suitable piece of wall or room for a hedge. A mixed hedge is better

for wildlife than one composed of just a single species. Of course, it won't look as neat but if you are reading this book, the chances are that this will not be an issue for you. A mix of Hawthorn, Blackthorn *Prunus spinosa*, Holly, Yew, *Viburnum tinus*, Elder *Sambucus nigra*, Spindle *Euonymous europaeus* and Dog Rose *Rosa canina* should provide birds with a decent choice of nesting cover, song posts and berries.

Nesting requirements of common garden birds

Species	Open/cavity nester	Height	Location
Blackbird	Open	<4m	Bush providing thick cover
Blue Tit	Cavity		Tree holes and nestboxes
Chaffinch	Open	1-4m	Canopy or fork of a bush
Coal Tit	Cavity		Tree holes and nestboxes
Dunnock	Open	15cm to 1.5m	Bush providing thick cover
Goldcrest	Open	2-12m	Conifer canopy
Goldfinch	Open	up to 15m	Bush or fork within tree canopy
Great Tit	Cavity		Tree holes and nestboxes
Greenfinch	Open	1-5m	Bush or creeper
Long-tailed Tit	Open		Bush providing thick cover
Mistle Thrush	Open	3-10m	Fork or bow of tree
Robin	Open	<3m	Bush providing thick cover
Song Thrush	Open	<4m	Bush providing thick cover
Spotted Flycatcher	Open/Cavity	<10m	Open cavity or crevice, in a creeper
Starling	Cavity	up to 15m	Cavity or nestbox
Tawny Owl	Cavity		Cavity or nestbox

A significant number of plants rely on birds to act as dispersal agents for their seeds. As an incentive, the plants often offer nutritious fleshy fruits to attract birds to take the seeds, hidden inside, and ingest them. The seeds have tough external coats that protect them from the digestive systems of birds, allowing them to be deposited elsewhere once they have passed through the bird's gut.

This apparently mutualistic arrangement (birds acting as dispersers and plants devoting resources to offering energetic rewards) is complicated by the fact that some birds eat the pulp and discard the seed (pulp-predators) or eat and digest the seed (seed-predators). Regardless of such considerations, there is plenty of evidence in the scientific literature to highlight those plants that are particularly valuable to birds as a source of fruits, berries or seeds (for ease of reading we will refer collectively to fruits, berries and arils as fruits).

Different fruits become available at particular times of the year, with some 'available' on the plant for a substantial period – perhaps because they are long-lasting or because they are only taken after more popular fruits are exhausted. Holly, in particular, has a long fruiting season. The first berries become available during September and the long-lasting fruits may remain on the tree through until the following July. Although one reason for this is the durability of the fruits, another is the fact that many Holly trees are defended by Mistle Thrushes, which prevents other birds from feeding on the fruits.

Fruiting season can vary across even closely-related plants. While *Sorbus aria* ripens in September, *Sorbus torminalis* ripens in November and *Sorbus aucuparia* ripens from late July. However, it is worth noting that *Sorbus aucuparia* has a more northerly range than the other two species and that plants in the northerly part of their British range tend to have fruit that ripens earlier than seen in their southern counterparts.

The nutritional characteristics of fruits may also vary with season, notably with water content of the pulp declining and average lipid content increasing as the season progresses. When

metabolised, lipids produce more energy (per gram of dry weight) than either protein or carbohydrates, the two other main nutritive components of the pulp.

Such differences may be related to the birds' needs; the plants effectively competing for seed dispersers and needing to have fruits that are as attractive as possible in order to secure dispersal. Individual bird species feeding on fruits will select those that offer the greatest returns for the effort spent in securing them. This may be influenced by the energy content of the fruits, their relative availability and ease of access. There is even evidence that birds actively select fruits with a high anthocyanin content. As well as being important pigments in ripe fruits, anthocyanins are well-known anti-oxidants. Fruits rich in anthocyanins are black or ultraviolet-reflecting (birds can see better in the UV spectrum than us). If plants use these anthocyanin pigments as an honest signal of the nutritional rewards on offer, then birds should preferentially select them.

Of course, not all the birds are after the nutritious pulp; others may be after the seeds themselves. Plants may seek to counter these avian cheats through the incorporation of toxic compounds into the seed coat or its lining. There is thus an evolutionary arms race in operation, with different factors coming into play, some seeking to attract particular seed dispersers, others seeking to prevent the actions of seed predators.

From a wildlife gardening point of view, we are simply interested in providing those fruit and berry producing

The seasonality of berry production

Strictly-speaking the fruiting year begins in late June, with the ripening of the year's first fruits. Among these, only Wild Cherry *Prunus avium* is taken by birds; domesticated varieties are also taken at this time. The last fruits are those of Ivy (from November).

Jun	Jul	Aug	Sep	Oct	Nov	Dec	Jan	Feb	Mar	Apr	May

Wild Cherry
Bird Cherry
Rowan
Hawthorn
Blackthorn
Buckthorn
Holly
Mistletoe
Hips
Guelder Rose
Ivy

Adapted from Snow & Snow (1988)

plants that attract and support particular species of bird. As such, we can use some of the evidence about feeding preferences and fruit availability to emerge from decades of research into this topic to draw up a list of suitable plants (see box on page 69).

Species preferences – A series of studies by Barbara & David Snow (see Resources) have highlighted the preferences of a number of familiar species. Blackbird was found to be rather catholic in its tastes, typically taking a range of fruits (including haws, rosehips, sloes, Dogwood, Buckthorn, Elder, Yew and Holly), though haws seemed to be the preferred fruit when choice was available. Song Thrush showed a clear preference for Yew, sloes, Elder and Guelder Rose and apparent avoidance of rosehips. The larger Mistle Thrush showed a strong preference for sloes over haws, while Redwing found sloes too large to tackle, preferring instead to feed on haws, a preference also shown by Fieldfare.

Only Blackbird, Fieldfare and Mistle Thrush were able to handle rosehips effectively, the hips being too large for the

Ash keys – Mike Toms

smaller Song Thrush and Redwing. Late in the fruiting season, when the choice is limited to Holly and Ivy, preference seems to be strongly towards Ivy, suggesting another reason why Holly berries may remain untouched until very late in the season.

Aliens and cultivated varieties – It is not just native species that produce fruit taken by birds. Introduced species and the cultivated varieties of native species may also produce suitable fruit. This is not always the case though. We have seen Garden Privet *Ligustrum ovalifolium* displayed in some lists as a suitable berry-producing plant for birds, yet this form does not produce fruit! Instead, plant Wild Privet *Ligustrum vulgare*, which produces beautiful black berries favoured by a range of bird species.

There has been a fair amount of debate over the different cultivars of some berry-producing shrubs (including those in the genus *Sorbus*) and how attractive they might be to birds. Since birds have been shown to use berry colour as an indicator of nutritive rewards, it seems sensible to assume that the differently-coloured varieties of these shrubs will differ in their attractiveness to birds. Ornamental fruits whose colours are not widely replicated within native fruits (for

Rosehips – Mike Toms

example white – seen only on Mistletoe) may prove less attractive to birds. This could explain why white-berried forms of *Sorbus* remain on the tree for so long.

Seeds and seed predators – The provision of seeds for birds can be as simple as leaving some of your flowers to set seed. Dead-heading your plants as soon as they have flowered will reduce the availability of such seeds and, while you may not want Dandelions and thistles seeding in your garden, you might be comfortable leaving your Lemon Balm to set seed. Goldfinches, in particular, will welcome the presence of such seeds. We would recommend leaving your annual tidy up of your herbaceous borders to as late in the year as possible (or preferably early the following year). Not only will this provide additional seed resources it will offer overwintering sites for insects.

Elder berries – Dawn Balmer

Other birds specialise in feeding on the larger seeds of many coniferous or deciduous trees. Siskins and Coal Tits depend on conifer seeds late in the year and when these seeds are in short supply they soon turn to garden feeding stations. The same is true of Bramblings and Chaffinches, though this time in relation to Beech mast. Of course, producing seed-bearing trees such as these is a very-long term commitment. As an alternative, try planting Alder (this favours wet soils) or Birch (favours dry or poor soils). These mature far more rapidly, are more manageable and will soon provide seeds for visiting Siskins and Lesser Redpolls.

Suitable berry-producing plants for birds

Bird Cherry *Prunus padus*, Blackberry *Rubus fruticosus* agg., Blackthorn *Prunus spinosa*, *Cotoneaster bullatus*, Cotoneaster 'cornubia' hybrids, *Cotonoeaster horizontalis*, Crab-apple *Malus sylvestris*, Dog Rose *Rosa canina*, Elder *Sambucus nigra*, Guelder Rose *Viburnum opulus*, Hawthorn *Crataegus monogyna*, Holly *Ilex aquifolium*, Honeysuckle *Lonicera periclymenon*, Ivy *Hedera helix*, Mezereon *Daphne mezereon*, Midland Hawthorn *Crataegus laevigata*, Mistletoe *Viscum album*, Perfoliate Honeysuckle *Lonicera caprifolium*, Oregon Grape *Mahonia aquifolium*, *Photinia davidiana*, *Pyracantha coccinea*, *Pyracantha rogersiana*, Rowan *Sorbus aucuparia*, Sea-buckthorn *Hippophae rhamnoides*, *Stranvaesia davidiana*, Wayfaring Tree *Viburnum lantana*, Whitebeam *Sorbus aria*, Wild Cherry *Prunus avium*, Wild Privet *Ligustrum vulgare*, Wild Service Tree *Sorbus torminalis*, Yew *Taxus baccata*.

Suitable seed-producing plants for birds

Alder *Alnus glutinosa*, Beech *Fagus sylvaticus*, Dandelion *Taraxacum* agg., Devil's-bit Scabious *Succisa pratensis*, Field Scabious *Knautia arvensis*, Greater Knapweed *Centaurea scabiosa*, Hazel *Corylus avellana*, Hornbeam *Carpinus betulus*, Lavender *Lavandula*, Lemon Balm *Melissa officinalis*, Silver Birch *Betula pendula*, Sunflower *Helianthus annuus*, Teasel *Dipsacus fullonum*, Thistles *Carduus/Cirsium*.

As we have seen in earlier sections of this book, insects and other invertebrates are an essential component of any wildlife garden. Very valuable in their own right, many also provide food for insectivorous birds. In this section, we look at how to attract insects into your garden, concentrating primarily on the more obvious groups, namely butterflies, moths and bumblebees.

One of the keys to maintaining a garden that is attractive to a wide range of insects and other invertebrates is the provision of pollen and nectar across as much of the year as possible. Fortunately, plants do not all flower at the same time; this means that the annual sequence of flowering times can be used as the basis for selecting particular plants for your garden. Do not equate flower size with value, since a big showy flower does not necessarily offer more rewards to a visiting insect than one that is much smaller and less showy. The small flowers of Holly on show in late spring are extremely well used by insects. Blossom is important for insects and other invertebrates, providing both nectar and pollen. Nectar is a sugar-based solution which provides a ready source of the carbohydrates needed to fuel insect flight. Pollen, which is rich in protein, is thought to be important for the production of insect eggs.

Flower form (see page 19) will influence the suitability of a plant for particular insects, with some nectar sources only available to those insects with particularly long tongues. Some plant cultivars provide little in the way of accessible nectar so it is important to select plants carefully, using lists of those known to be accessible to particular species (see boxes over the following pages). As a general rule, native species will tend to support nectar feeders better than introduced species. However, there are some really valuable introduced plants that either deliver large quantities of nectar or provide it during that part of the year when other sources of nectar are in short supply.

Female Orange-tip – Mike Toms

Butterflies and moths – Although a good-sized and well-positioned garden in the south of England may be visited by 20 or more species of butterfly and 200 or more species of moth, most of us will receive visits from significantly fewer species than this. Many of those species that do visit will simply be passing through or visiting the garden in search of nectar, all the while breeding in other nearby habitats. Having said this, it is important not to underestimate the value of a good wildlife garden for butterflies and moths. With increasing pressure on other habitats and the loss of nectaring opportunities elsewhere, gardens may be one of the few places with nectar available throughout the year. Such nectar sources are of particular importance early in the season, especially for the small number of butterflies which overwinter as adults (these include Brimstone, Small Tortoiseshell, Peacock, Comma and, more recently, Red Admiral).

Gardens may also be used for breeding, with a significant number of both butterfly and moth species known to use common garden plants as food for their developing caterpillars (see box below). By providing both suitable nectaring and food plant opportunities,

Food plants for caterpillars of some common butterflies

Many butterflies use a range of cues (including plant species, degree of shade, leaf size, microclimate and plant condition) to determine where to lay their eggs. While you might have the right plant it might be in the wrong place and it can prove tricky to meet their exacting requirements. This, and the fact that nettles are a common species elsewhere, may explain why it is so difficult to attract breeding butterflies to a garden nettle patch.

Holly Blue – Mike Toms

Small Skipper	Yorkshire Fog *Holcus lanatus*
Large Skipper	Cock's-foot *Dactylis glomerata*
Brimstone	Buckthorn* *Rhamnus cathartica*, Alder Buckthorn* *Frangula alnus*
Large White	Brassicas, Nasturtium *Tropaeolum majus*
Small White	Brassicas, Nasturtium *Tropaeolum majus*, Hedge Mustard *Sisymbrium officinale*
Green-veined White	Garlic Mustard *Alliaria petiolata*, Cuckooflower *Cardamine pratensis*
Orange-tip	Cuckooflower *Cardamine pratensis*, Garlic Mustard *Alliaria petiolata*, Honesty *Lunaria annua*, Dame's-violet *Hesperis matronalis*
Small Copper	Common Sorrel *Rumex acetosa*, Sheep's Sorrel *Rumex acetosella*
Common Blue	Common Bird's-foot-trefoil *Lotus corniculatus*
Holly Blue	Holly *Ilex aquifolium*, Ivy *Hedera helix*, Spindle *Euonymus europaeus*
Red Admiral	Common Nettle *Urtica dioica*, Small Nettle *Urtica urens*, Pellitory-of-the-wall *Parietaria judaica*, Hop *Humulus lupulus*
Painted Lady	Thistles *Cirsium* spp. and *Carduus* spp., mallows *Malva* spp.
Small Tortoiseshell	Common Nettle *Urtica dioica*, Small Nettle *Urtica urens*
Peacock	Common Nettle *Urtica dioica*
Comma	Common Nettle *Urtica dioica*, Hop *Humulus lupulus*, currants *Ribes* spp.
Speckled Wood	Cock's-foot *Dactylis glomerata*, Yorkshire-fog *Holcus lanatus*
Gatekeeper	Various grasses, including bents *Agrostis* spp. and fescues *Festuca* spp.
Meadow Brown	Various grasses, including bents *Agrostis* spp. and fescues *Festuca* spp.

* all parts of these species are poisonous

you should be able to attract a range of different species. The key to success is understanding which butterflies and moths visit which flowers and why.

Researchers have discovered that butterflies forage in a way that maximises their energy returns while, at the same time, minimises the amount of energy they spend whilst foraging. Generally, butterflies that weigh more (and are less-efficient fliers) forage on plants that produce massed flowers, only bothering with solitary flowers if they are unusually rich in nectar. This strategy reduces foraging costs. Such butterflies also tend to have longer tongues and are able to access flowers where the nectar is tucked away at the end of a long tube (known as the corolla). A deep corolla restricts the clientele to long-tongued species and this means that there is likely to be more nectar available in such flowers because fewer insects are feeding on it. The same researchers also found that butterflies do not forage on flowers where the depth of the corolla is greater than the length of their tongue.

Nearly all of the plants visited by butterflies are perennials, presumably because these offer greater rewards. This all suggests that you should provide plants like *Buddleja davidii*, Red Campion *Silene dioica*, *Hebe* spp. and even *Agapanthus praecox* for the longer-tongued butterflies (Painted Lady, Red Admiral, Peacock and

Nectar sources

Dandelion *Taraxacum officinale* agg., Hemp-agrimony *Eupatorium cannabinum*, knapweeds *Centaurea* spp., Wild Marjoram *Origanum vulgare*, Goat Willow *Salix caprea*, Field Scabious *Knautia arvensis*, Devil's-bit Scabious *Succisa pratensis*, Ivy *Hedera helix*, Spear Thistle *Cirsium vulgare*, Water Mint *Mentha aquatica*, *Buddleja davidii*, *Buddleja* x *weyeriana*, French Marigold *Tagetes patula*, Ice Plant *Sedum spectabile*, Lavender *Lavandula angustifolia*, Michaelmas-daisy *Aster novae-angliae*, Red Valerian *Centranthus ruber*, Blackberry *Rubus fruticosus* agg., *Verbena bonariensis*, Globe Thistle *Echinops ritro* and various thymes *Thymus* spp.

Small Tortoiseshell). The shortest-tongued species, like the skippers, Gatekeeper and Common Blue will need flowers like those of Bramble *Rubus fruticosus* agg., Ice Plant *Sedum spectabile*, Hemp-agrimony *Eupatorium cannabinum*, Common Ragwort *Senecio jacobaea* and Shasta Daisy *Leucanthemum* x *superbum*.

When it comes to suitable nectar sources for butterflies it is not just which species you plant that is important but also their location. Butterflies much prefer to feed in sunny, sheltered parts of the garden, with scented blooms presented in large and visible displays. Try to plant species of similar height together and look at the different growth forms to make sure that the butterflies can access the flowers. Also consider your pruning regime. For example, if you have several *Buddleja davidii* in your garden, prune them in sequence through February, March and April. This should extend the flowering season of this plant in your garden. You can even try giving one bush a light trim in June to remove the flower buds, forcing it to flower very late (possibly up until October). Another useful set of late-season plants are the

A skipper on Bramble – Mike Toms

various Michaelmas-daisies, especially *Aster novae-belgii* and *Aster novae-angliae*, since many varieties extend flowering into October. They also suit most soil types and are fairly vigorous.

Most moths visit flowers at night, feeding in a similar manner to butterflies but with some differences in their preferences. For example, the ball-shaped flowers of *Buddleja globosa* are well used by moths but seem less attractive to butterflies. Other plants, such as Red Valerian *Centranthus rubra* and Goat Willow *Salix caprea* are well used by both. Moths seem particularly attracted to those plants which produce their scent in the evening, such as honeysuckle *Lonicera* spp., Jasmine *Jasminum officinale*, Common Evening-primrose *Oenothera biennis* and Dame's-violet *Hesperis matronalis*. Early season nectar is equally important for moths, with Goat Willow well used by Early Grey, Quaker and Red Chestnut moths. Late-season nectar, notably that of Ivy *Hedera helix*, is used by the Chestnut, a common resident moth.

You have a better chance of getting a range of moth species to breed in your garden than you do butterflies and many may breed unnoticed. It will tend to be the more common and widespread species that do breed but, with widespread declines in the wider countryside, anything you can do to help is really positive. Look at which plants provide for a good range of moth species, decide if they will work in your garden then off you go!

Some food plants for moth caterpillars

We have an excellent understanding of the food plants used by the caterpillars of many of our larger moths, highlighting the wide range of species supported by plants like Lady's Bedstraw, Bilberry and Hawthorn. The figure in brackets shows the number of larger moth species known to use the plant.

Berberis spp. (13), Lady's Bedstraw *Galium verum* (30), Bilberry *Vaccinium myrtillus* (55), Common Bird's-foot-trefoil *Lotus corniculatus* (27), Bramble *Rubus fruticosus* agg. (61), *Buddleja* spp. (3), Red Campion *Silene dioica* (9), White Clover *Trifolium repens* (13), Lawson's Cypress *Chamaecyparis lawsoniana* (10), dandelions *Taraxacum* spp. (67), dead-nettles *Lamium* spp. (17), docks *Rumex* spp. (95), dogwoods *Cornus* spp. (9), Foxglove *Digitalis purpurea* (9), goldenrods *Solidago* spp. (21), hawthorns *Crataegus* spp. (115), Hazel *Corylus avellana* (72), Hemp-agrimony *Eupatorum cannabinum* (10), honeysuckles *Lonicera* spp. (30), Ivy *Hedera helix* (16), Marjoram *Origanum vulgare* (9), Meadowsweet *Filipendula ulmaria* (16), nettles *Urtica* spp. (30), oaks *Quercus* spp. (130), pinks *Dianthus* spp. (7), plums *Prunus* spp. (35), Primrose *Primula vulgaris* (21), privets *Ligustrum* spp. (24), Purple Loosestrife *Lythrum salicaria* (5), Ragged Robin *Lychnis flos-cuculi* (4), rock-roses *Helianthemum* spp. (7), roses *Rosa* spp. (40), Rowan *Sorbus aucuparia* (20), st. John's-worts *Hypericum* spp. 8), scabious: *Knautia*, *Scabiosa* and *Succisa* (9), Common Sorrel *Rumex acetosa* (13), Sheep's Sorrel *Rumex acetosella* (9), Wild Strawberry *Fragaria vesca* (12), Thrift *Armeria maritima* (9), thymes *Thymus* spp. (9), Traveller's-joy *Clematis vitalba* (14), Horsehoe Vetch *Hippocrepis comosa* (3), Kidney Vetch *Anthyllis vulneraria* (6), Yarrow *Achillea millefolium* (16), Yew *Taxus baccata* (4).

After Crafer (2005)

Bumblebees – Flowers are of great importance to bumblebees, providing a place to shelter from inclement weather and meeting their nutritional requirements in the form of pollen and nectar, the latter also providing an important source of water.

Although bumblebees have been recorded feeding on a wide range of flowers, some are clearly more bee-friendly than others. As with butterflies and many other insects, flower form is all-important and the heavily-modified blooms created by plant breeders, are often unsuitable. Double-flowered varieties and most annual bedding plants fall into the unsuitable category.

Research studies have revealed complex relationships between bumblebees and flowers and we have a good understanding of which species are most heavily used at different times of the year. Many of the flowers visited by bumblebees are suited to their relatively long tongues but there is quite a bit of variation in tongue length, both between different species and within a species. This means that it is important to grow a range of different plant species, selected to get a balance of flower forms (for example, brush-type flowers like those of various mints and sallows, gullet-type flowers like Foxglove and dead-nettles and bell-shaped flowers like bindweed and the bellflowers) and flowering seasons (see box on page 75).

Some plant species attract visits from a number of bumblebee species (for example Red Clover *Trifolium pratense* and Common Bird's-foot-trefoil *Lotus corniculatus*), while others are used by just one or two species. Similarly, some bumblebee species visit a range of plants, others restrict their attentions to plants from just a small number of families. Both native plants and related introductions or cultivated forms may be used though it is often preferable to use the native form. For example, some cultivated varieties of Foxglove are thought to produce little nectar so sticking to the native purple form is recommended.

Queen Ruderal Bumblebee – Dave Goulson

Nectar and pollen sources used by bumblebees

Although not an exhaustive list, the following suggestions should give you quite a bit of choice when it comes to suitable plants for bumblebees (as well as Honey Bees and other solitary bees). Additional advice may be sought from the Bumblebee Conservation Trust (see Resources) who have produced a very useful booklet on the subject of gardening for bumblebees. This also includes advice on providing nesting opportunities.

March–April

Apples *Malus domestica*, *Berberis* spp., Bleeding-heart *Dicentra formosa*, Bluebell *Hyacinthoides non-scripta*, cherries *Prunus* spp., Dandelion *Taraxacum officinale* agg., currant *Ribes* spp., Goat Willow *Salix caprea*, Ground-ivy *Glechoma hedeacea*, Lungwort *Pulmonaria officinalis*, *Mahonia* spp., Rosemary *Rosmarinus officinalis*, Red Dead-nettle *Lamium purpureum*, White Dead-nettle *Lamium album*, Winter Heath *Erica carnea*.

May–June

Aquilegia spp., Borage *Borago officinalis*, *Buddleja globosa*, Bugle *Ajuga reptans*, *Campanula* spp., *Ceanothus* spp., Chives *Allium schoenoprasum*, Common Bistort *Persicaria bistorta*, Common Comfrey *Sympytum officinale*, *Geranium* spp., Foxglove *Digitalis purpurea*, *Hebe* spp., Honeywort *Cerinthe major* 'Purpurascens', Kidney Vetch *Anthyllis vulneraria*, Lupin *Lupinus* x *regalis*, Red Campion *Silene dioica*, Red Clover *Trifolium pratense*, Selfheal *Prunella vulgaris*, Wallflower *Erysimum cheiri*, White Clover *Trifolium repens*, Field Woundwort *Stachys arvensis*, Yellow Rattle *Rhinanthus minor*.

July–August

Bramble *Rubus fruticosus* agg., burdocks *Arctium* spp., Black Horehound *Ballota nigra*, *Buddleja davidii*, Cat-mint *Nepeta cataria*, Common Bird's-foot-trefoil *Lotus corniculatus*, Common Hemp-nettle *Galeopsis tetrahit*, Common Knapweed *Centaurea nigra*, Cornflower *Centaurea cyanus*, *Delphinium elatum*, Globe-thistles *Echinops exaltatus*, *Echinops ritro*, *Echinops bannaticus*, Great Mullein *Verbascum thapsus*, Hollyhock *Alcea rosea*, Iceplant *Sedum spectabile*, Lavender *Lavandula angustifolia*, Meadow Clary *Salvia pratensis*, nasturtiums, Rosebay Willowherb *Chamerion angustifolium*, Sainfoin *Onobrychis viciifolia*, Devil's-bit Scabious *Succisa pratensis*, thistles *Cirsium/Carduus*, Tufted Vetch *Vicia cracca*, Viper's-bugloss *Echium vulgare*, Water Mint *Mentha aquatica*, Wild Marjoram *Origanum vulgare*.

Other invertebrates – While butterflies, moths and bumblebees are some of our most obvious and attractive invertebrates they are certainly not the only ones to use our gardens. There are likely to be many thousands of different invertebrates in a typical garden, the vast majority of them living out their lives completely unnoticed by the likes of your average gardener (even one interested in wildlife). If we are largely unaware of their existence you may ask how we can expect to manage our gardens in a way that will benefit them.

The truth is that most of these invertebrates are present not because of our activities but in spite of them. However, there are things that we can do to make our gardens even better (see box). The provision of nectar and pollen sources (already highlighted for butterflies and bees) will also benefit many other inverterbrates, from pollen beetles to hoverflies and the crab spiders that prey on flower-feeding insects. Similarly, use of plants for structure and nesting cover, or to provide berries for visiting thrushes, will also have a knock-on benefit for other wildlife. Finally, it is worth noting that certain invertebrate groups are highly beneficial in the garden. For example, hoverflies, lacewings and ladybirds all help to control the numbers of perceived pest species, so why not encourage them to help keep things in balance?

A *Platycheirus* hoverfly – Mike Toms

How to help

Chemicals: Avoid using chemicals in the garden. The use of insecticides, molluscicides and herbicides to target a particular problem will inevitably have a knock-on impact on non-target plants and animals. As we have seen in other sections of the book, there are ways to manage pest and disease issues without the need to resort to chemicals.

Feeding opportunities: The range of food sources used by invertebrates is as diverse as the range of invertebrates itself. Whole communities may be dependent upon the thatch in your lawn, the decaying pile of wood by your shed or the bark mulch on your flowerbed. Maximise invertebrate diversity by increasing the number of microhabitats within your garden.

Shelter: It is not just log piles that provide shelter; leaving dead flowerheads *in situ* through the winter months will provide overwintering opportunities for many invertebrates, as will leaving fallen leaves and timber. The key is not to be too tidy-minded. You can also provide new opportunities by building or buying shelters. Some of the best are simple contructions of hollow canes held together in a bundle and placed in suitable sheltered parts of the garden.

Breeding sites: Again, a diversity of microhabitats should provide suitable breeding sites for a range of species. You can also provide opportunities for particular species, perhaps by investing in a mason bee nesting kit. Positioned in a warm, south-facing location such kits can prove very successful. Bumblebee nesting boxes on the other hand have a very low success rate.

Foods and feeding

There is no question that the provision of supplementary food attracts wild birds into our gardens. Research carried out by the BTO has shown that the chances of 24 bird species occurring in gardens was significantly higher at sites where food was provided than it was at sites with no such provision.

The range of foods on offer, now much wider than it once was, will ultimately influence which species visit your garden feeding station. The introduction of new foods, such as sunflower hearts, high-energy seed mixes and nyjer seed, has led to the increasing use of garden feeding stations by species that were once infrequent visitors. A good example of this is the Goldfinch, a species that has greatly increased its use of feeding stations over the last couple of decades, thanks to a change in our provisioning habits.

The volume of food provided at Britain's bird tables is staggering; the bird feeding industry is now worth somewhere in the region of £200 million annually.

Make a difference – There is a wealth of scientific literature demonstrating the positive effects that supplementary feeding can have on wild birds. Studies have shown how it can influence overwinter survival, breeding success and the timing of breeding. Although much of this work has been in habitats other than gardens, similar principles apply and it is clear from the way in which birds use our gardens that the provision of supplementary food has a role to play in their annual cycle.

When and where to feed – Both the BTO and RSPB advocate the provision of appropriate foods throughout the year, and not just during winter. During late spring and the breeding season, many birds may find it difficult to locate enough food to feed both themselves and their chicks. In many species the growing chicks are fed on invertebrates, the parents only taking supplementary food for themselves. Although adult birds appear able to differentiate between different types of food, and to select appropriate food for their young, some studies have shown that they will also

Goldfinch feeding on black sunflower seeds – John Harding

deliver food provided at local bird tables to the nest. The evidence suggests, in Great Tits and Blue Tits at least, that the parent birds may feed their chicks on the supplementary foods when favoured chick foods are in short supply. This means that consideration needs to be given to which foods are provided. For example, whole loose peanuts (which could choke young chicks) should be avoided and we would recommend that these are only ever provided behind a wire mesh. Other foods that should be avoided are those with a high salt content (salted peanuts and bacon rind), those which may swell up inside the bird (desiccated coconut), those which are mouldy or spoiled and those which may harbour bacteria (*e.g.* meat scraps). More advice on feeding can be found in the series of BTO leaflets on garden birds (see the Resources section).

What to feed

Provision of a range of different foods, presented in different ways (*e.g.* hanging feeders, bird tables, on the ground) is the best way to attract a wide range of birds to your garden. In addition to the foods listed below you might like to try finely-grated cheese, sultanas (though note that these are toxic to dogs), peanut cake, windfall apples and fat smeared into cracks in tree bark.

Black sunflower seed, introduced in the early 1990s, has revolutionised bird feeding by providing a high energy food in a readily accessible form. Black sunflower seeds have thinner shells than the traditional striped sunflower seeds and so are a favourite with Greenfinches and tits, though they may be shunned if hearts are available. Cheaper than hearts but they make more mess.

Sunflower hearts are more expensive than the black sunflower seeds but they have two advantages. First, the birds can feed more quickly because they do not have to remove the husk. Second, the lack of a husk means that there are no unsightly piles of husks left behind on the ground after the birds have fed. Hearts go down well with House Sparrows, Greenfinches, Chaffinches and the tits.

Seed mixes come in a vast range, differing in content and quality. Cheap mixes often have a high proportion of cereal and attract pigeons. Better quality mixes are lower in cereal content and so are particularly suitable for finches and buntings. The best mixes are carefully balanced to cater for a range of species. With seed mixes you tend to get what you pay for.

Nyjer seed is a relatively new introduction to the bird feeding market and it is one that has found favour with Goldfinches, which seem to like the small size of these seeds. Because they are so small, nyjer seeds need to be supplied in a specially adapted feeder. They are oil rich and ideal for birds with delicate bills.

Peanuts are high in the oils and proteins needed by birds and have been used for many years. Always buy good quality peanuts from a reputable source and avoid those that show any signs of mould. Quality peanuts, such as those endorsed by the BTO, RSPB, Birdcare Standards Association or sold by CJ WildBird Foods Ltd, will have been tested for a naturally occurring poison called aflatoxin. Peanuts are best supplied behind a mesh.

Hygiene and disease

Outbreaks of disease may occur in populations of wild birds wherever they occur, including those visiting gardens. Among the most well known of these are those caused by *Salmonella*, *E.coli* and, more recently, *Trichomonas gallinae*, all of which have been recorded from birds visiting garden feeding stations. Although precise symptoms may vary between diseases (and between bird species and individual birds), there are some general symptoms that may alert you to the occurrence of disease in the population of birds visiting your garden. Affected birds often appear lethargic, reluctant to move away from the feeding station, fluffed up and show difficulty in swallowing food and/or water. Research has established that transmission rates are typically increased where birds gather together in large numbers, with contaminated food and water providing the pathways by which disease can spread from one individual to another. The following guidance should help you reduce the risk of disease transmission.

Feeding station layout – Since the risk of disease transmission is related to the numbers of birds congregating together, it is best to use several feeding sites within your garden rather than place all your feeders in one spot. This will serve to disperse the feeding birds over a larger area. It is also essential that you move your feeding sites around periodically, allowing areas to 'rest' and, by doing so, reducing the risk of contamination.

Feeder design – Hanging seed feeders typically retain the food within a clear plastic tube and this means that there is a very low risk of the food becoming contaminated by droppings or saliva. Bird tables, where birds stand on and amongst the food, carry a greater risk of contamination. However, whilst this implies that hanging feeders are better from a disease prevention point of view, it is worth remembering that many species are unable to use hanging feeders and that, with good hygiene practice, bird tables should be just as safe. Look for a feeder that keeps food dry and reduces the risk of contamination.

Keeping things clean – The regular cleaning and disinfecting of bird tables, bird baths and hanging feeders is an important component of good hygiene practice. Feeding equipment should be disinfected on a regular (weekly or fortnightly) basis, using an appropriate disinfectant (such as Tamodine-E or Ark-klens) followed by thorough rinsing and air-drying before re-use. Rubber gloves should be worn for the purpose, and hands and forearms should be washed thoroughly after handling or cleaning feeders. You may find it useful to double-up on feeding equipment, so that one set is air-drying after cleaning while the other is in use. The same is true for bird baths, which should also be cleaned on a regular cycle. The ground beneath feeding stations should be kept clean through regular sweeping and by being disinfected with Gardenklens

Greenfinch – John Harding

powder. Get into the practice of gauging how much food you put out each day to match what the birds are taking, especially on bird tables, so that there is no food hanging around which can become contaminated.

Food safety – Source your bird food from reputable suppliers and store it in a clean, dry and cool environment inaccessible to pests. This will minimise the risk of fungal or bacterial contamination and will also avoid encouraging rats and mice.

Sick birds – If you keep a close eye on your visiting birds you may very occasionally spot a bird that appears unwell. Unfortunately, because treatment in the wild is usually ineffective, by the time that you are able to catch a sick bird for treatment by a veterinarian, it is likely to be too late. This means that it is best to take preventative action to stop an outbreak from occurring in the first place.

One often-asked question is whether to cease feeding altogether if you spot a diseased bird visiting your feeding station. If, by ceasing feeding, the birds are likely to disperse to feed at lower densities elsewhere then it may be sensible to cease feeding for a short period (perhaps two-three weeks). However, if you are confident in your own hygiene practices then it may be best to continue feeding,

particularly if you suspect that the birds would simply move to another garden feeding station locally where the various hygiene measures outlined here are not followed. If in doubt, seek further advice from the BTO or UFAW (see Resources).

Diseases of garden birds

SALMONELLOSIS: This is most commonly caused by the bacterium *Salmonella typhimurium*. Most outbreaks of this disease are reported from December–April, with transmission thought to be via faecal contamination of food. *Symptons*: Fluffed-up, lethargic, difficulty swallowing.

COLIBACILLOSIS: Caused by the bacterium *E.coli*. Most reports of the disease occur from March–May. Again, faecal contamination of food appears to be the main route of disease transmission. *Symptons*: Fluffed-up, lethargic, difficulty swallowing.

TRICHOMONOSIS: Caused by a trichomonad parasite and first noted in finches in 2005. Most reports occur during late summer. Salival contamination of food and water is the main route of disease transmission. *Symptons*: Fluffed-up, lethargic, difficulty swallowing, wet around beak.

GROWTHS ON LEGS AND FEET: Various causes, including Fringilla papillomavirus (in Chaffinches), bacterial infections, mites and other viruses. *Symptons*: All produce similar looking swellings, which may vary in size from small nodules to larger warts that engulf the whole leg and foot.

Nestboxing for birds

Nesting opportunities are often lacking in gardens, especially those associated with the presence of natural cavities. Adding a nestbox can offer a quick solution to this problem.

Design and position – Nestbox designs fall into three main categories; the classic hole-fronted box (often used for tits), the open-fronted box (Spotted Flycatcher and Robin) and various specialist designs for species like House Martin and Swift. All can be equally effective, although correct placement of the box and the presence of other resources needed by the birds are clearly important. Ideally a nestbox should be positioned such that the entrance faces towards the northeast quadrant, *i.e.* away from prevailing wind and rain. It should be positioned among some suitable cover and out of strong sunlight. Never place a nestbox next to a bird table or hanging feeders. Position the nestbox so that it is not disturbed, perhaps in a quiet part of the garden. Height is less important than you might imagine but the box is usually best placed six or more feet off the ground.

Construction and maintenance – With so many good designs on the market, it is often easiest to purchase a box ready constructed. Make sure that you know which species you intend to attract and then check that the box you are about to purchase meets the bird's requirements (see box). Avoid those designs that have been put together with the emphasis on visual appearance rather than functionality. Some may be far too small, while others may be poorly constructed, exposing the occupants to the elements. Building your own nestbox can be particularly rewarding and there are a number of good books on the subject, including the BTO Nestbox Guide by Chris du Feu (see Resources).

Try not to disturb your nesting birds unless you are participating in the Nest Record Scheme (see BTO – Resources) but do clean the box out at the end of the year (between 1st August and 31st January) to reduce the build-up of nest parasites that may deter birds from using the box the following year. Check that the box remains in good condition and is still firmly fixed to whatever you have attached it to.

Nestlings in a nestbox – Mike Toms

When constructing a nestbox, use wood that is at least 15mm thick and suitable for use outside. In order to prolong its life, you may wish to treat the outside of the box with a coat of wood preservative. Avoid traditional oil-based preservatives but go instead for one of the non-toxic, water-based preservatives that are now on the market.

Blue Tit: Hole-fronted box; Size: base 150 x 120mm, front 150 x 175mm. Entrance hole: 25mm. Siting: 1-5m off ground, with clear flight path to nest entrance. 7–16 eggs, incubation 13–14 days, nestling 18–19 days.

Great Tit: Hole-fronted box; Size: base 150 x 120mm, front 150 x 175mm. Entrance hole: 28mm. Siting: 1-5m off ground, with clear flight path to nest entrance. 5–12 eggs, incubation 12–16 days, nestling 18–24 days.

Coal Tit: Hole-fronted box; Size: base 150 x 120mm, front 150 x 175mm. Entrance hole: 25mm. Siting: low, will nest higher if no competition for nest site. 7–11 eggs, incubation 13–14 days, nestling 16–17 days.

House Sparrow: Hole-fronted box; Size: base 150 x 120mm, front 150 x 175mm. Entrance hole: 32mm. Siting: 2–5m off ground, fixed to tree or building. 3–6 eggs, incubation 9–18 days, nestling 11–19 days.

Tree Sparrow: Hole-fronted box; Size: base 150 x 120mm, front 150 x 175mm. Entrance hole: 28mm. Siting: 2–5m off ground, avoid disturbed sites. 4–6 eggs, incubation 12–14 days, nestling 12–15 days.

Nuthatch: Hole-fronted box; Size: base 150 x 120mm, front 150 x 175mm. Entrance hole: 32mm. Siting: >3m off ground, with clear flight path to entrance. 6–9 eggs, incubation 14–15 days, nestling 23–25 days.

Starling: Hole-fronted box; Size: base 150 x 180mm, front 150 x 250mm. Entrance hole: 45mm. Siting: >2.5m off ground, on tree trunk or building. 4–7 eggs, incubation 12–14 days, nestling 20–22 days.

Jackdaw: Hole-fronted box; Size: base 300 x 300mm, front 300 x 400mm. Entrance hole: 150mm. Siting: at least 3m off ground, but as high as possible. 4–6 eggs, incubation 17–18 days, nestling 30–35 days.

Robin: Open-fronted box; Size: base 150 x 120mm, front 150 x 100mm. Siting: 1-3m off ground, well-hidden by thick vegetation. 5–7 eggs, incubation 12–14 days, nestling 12–15 days.

Wren: Open-fronted box; Size: base 150 x 120mm, front 150 x 140mm. Siting: 1-3m off ground, well hidden by thick vegetation. 5–6 eggs, incubation 14–15 days, nestling 16–17 days.

Spotted Flycatcher: Open-fronted box; Size: base 150 x 120mm, front 150 x 60mm. Siting: 2-4m off ground, with clear outlook. 4–5 eggs, incubation 12–14 days, nestling 12–15 days.

Red in tooth and claw

Nature is red in tooth and claw, with the complex interactions between predators and their prey acted out on a daily basis in our gardens. Much of this predation goes unnoticed – for example, the small insectivorous birds predating aphids, caterpillars and tiny flies. However, where the act of predation involves higher organisms (such as when a Sparrowhawk kills a Woodpigeon) it often catches our attention. While many welcome the sight of a Sparrowhawk in their garden as a sign of a healthy environment, others are distressed by the grizzly struggle that typically ensues.

Sparrowhawk – William Logan

It is important to understand that Sparrowhawks, Magpies and other native predators have evolved alongside the species upon which they prey. As such, complex interactions work both ways, with the availability of prey often limiting the size of the predator population. To date, despite a number of high profile studies, no evidence has been found to support the notion (held by some) that recovery of the Sparrowhawk population or, indeed, the increase in the Magpie population, has brought about any of the declines seen in our farmland and woodland birds. Instead, changes in the nature of the habitats within which these birds live appear to be behind many of the declines.

Of course, some of the predators using gardens are not native species but have either been introduced (*e.g.* Grey Squirrel) or are kept as pets (*e.g.* cat). There is evidence of an effect of Grey Squirrel predation on the breeding success of certain woodland birds and it may well be that Grey Squirrels act in a similar manner within the built environment. We know, from various scientific studies, that cats may be responsible for up to one-third of the mortality occurring in certain local populations of particular bird species (Churcher & Lawton 1987) and that cats can have a markedly adverse impact on bird populations living on remote islands. We also have a national estimate, admittedly derived from the scaling up of local figures, of the number of birds killed annually by cats. This figure is estimated at some 25-29 million individuals. While such figures might suggest that cat predation has a serious and significant influence on prey populations, it may be that cat predation is compensatory (with cats taking birds that would have died from other causes, notably starvation, in the following months) rather than additive (*i.e.* predation is additional to other mortality causes). The most recent study to look at the effects of cat predation failed to find any clear link between urban cat densities and the richness or density of bird species. This suggests that more work is needed before we can be sure of the scale and implications of this type of predation.

One often heard comment from those feeding garden birds is that they feel that by feeding the birds they are putting them at increased risk of predation. While this may be true if viewed in isolation, it is worth noting that research has demonstrated that birds are able to weigh-up the risks of being predated and balance this against the risks of starvation if they do not utilise a particular feeding opportunity. This is why we see adult/dominant birds feeding on those bird feeders positioned closest to cover, effectively pushing immature/subordinate individuals out onto the more exposed feeders where the risk of predation is higher. Predation risk is also one of the factors contributing to the daily pattern of feeder use, shaping how and when small birds visit feeding stations over the course of the day.

Tipping the balance – There are various ways in which you can make your garden, and in particular the area around your feeding station, less suitable for predators. By doing so it is possible to tip the balance of predation risk in favour of the prey. One of the most effective options is to position bird tables away from low cover (where cats may hide) but close to taller shrubs and bushes to give small birds the opportunity to dive into cover should a predatory Sparrowhawk

appear. Sparrowhawks like to use the available cover in order to get as close to their prey as possible. As such, you will often see them work along the blind side of hedgerow or fence, flipping up and over at just the point where the feeding station is positioned. Move your feeding station around the garden on a regular basis and the Sparrowhawk will not be able to predict where the smaller birds will be feeding.

Greenfinches asserting who has the right to feed on a choice feeder – Jill Pakenham

The effects of cat predation may also be minimised by careful positioning of the feeding station, avoiding parts of the garden where there is dense low cover in which cats may hide. There are various cat deterrents on the market, some of which appear to work better than others. A sonic device, triggering an unpleasant sound when a cat crosses in front of it, may be one option, though this needs to be moved around the garden periodically to ensure the cat does not simply avoid that route.

If you are the owner of a cat yourself, then consider what you can do to reduce its impact on the local bird, mammal and amphibian population. The addition of two bells to the collar can reduce the effectiveness of your cat as a hunter of small birds, but has no impact on its ability to catch other wildlife. Also consider keeping your cat indoors overnight or if you have young, inexperienced, birds in the garden.

Other risks

There are other risks faced by those birds using our gardens, some physical and others chemical in nature. As with predators, a common sense approach is likely to provide a worthwhile solution, enabling you to minimise the risks and, by doing so, help your garden birds.

Slug pellets – Although a number of non-chemical methods exist for the control of slugs within the garden environment (see page 28), many gardeners still resort to the use of slug pellets. Concerns have been expressed over the use of these chemicals in relation to their impact on non-target organisms (notably Hedgehog and Song Thrush). The available scientific evidence supports the view that Hedgehogs may be adversely affected by slug pellets and there are a number of cases where individual Hedgehogs have died as a direct result of molluscicide poisoning.

Changes in the survival rates of young Song Thrushes are sufficient to have driven the decline seen in this species since the 1970s. Since the use of molluscicides is one of the candidates for driving these changes, it would seem prudent to avoid using slug pellets within the garden. It is worth noting that each year a number of pets die from eating slug pellets and there are cases where children have ingested them.

Song Thrush – Jill Pakenham

Other garden chemicals
– Insecticides used to control plant pests are almost invariably non-specific, killing a range of beneficial insects and other non-target species. Even organically-approved pesticides (for example those based on Pyrethrum) may harm beneficial insects and our recommendation would be to use such chemicals only as a last resort. Consider other alternatives to minimise pest and disease outbreaks: companion planting, good hygiene, crop rotation, careful selection of varieties, physical barriers and promotion of beneficial insects.

Netting – Netting used for fruit cages and to protect vegetable beds may sometimes result in birds becoming trapped. Therefore, it is important to make regular checks of fruit cages and other netting to ensure that no birds or other species have become trapped. Do not leave netting piled up in a heap in a place where birds might come into contact with it.

Windows – A significant number of birds die each year through collision with windows. A study of window strikes, carried out by the BTO, suggests that such collisions normally result from one of three things. First, a bird may see through a pair of opposing windows and wrongly assume that it can fly straight through. Second, a bird may see the sky or a bush reflected in a window and fly towards it (see the photograph above for a good example of this). Finally, a bird may be spooked into a window by the approach of a predator or some other perceived risk.

The latter case is often associated with the presence of a bird table or hanging feeders quite close to the window such that, when spooked, the birds fail to spot the window in their efforts to escape. Moving the feeding station further away from the window can help reduce this problem. Another option is to help the birds spot the window in the first place. Net curtains seem to work well (especially for reducing fly-through strikes) but they may be less effective for those collisions caused by a reflection. An alternative approach is to use sentinels – stickers that attach to the window, often in the shape of a spider web or the outline of a bird of prey. These seem to work well, though not in all cases. Interestingly, it appears that dirty windows attract fewer window strikes than clean ones!

Results from the BTO study also indicated that the average number of window strikes was significantly higher for patio doors than it was for other types of window. This may stem from a combination of their size, the fact that being double-glazed means they tend to be highly reflective and because many people place their feeding station outside their patio windows.

Water butts – Results from the Garden Bird Health initiative highlight the dangers that uncovered water butts pose to birds. All containers should have their lids fitted or, if not being used to store water (*e.g.* a bucket), they should be stored on their side to avoid any risk to birds and other wildlife.

Hedges and nesting birds – The maintenance of hedges through cutting is something that may cause problems for nesting birds if carried out at the wrong time of the year. Traditionally, hedgerows are cut in late autumn or early spring, the work completed before the new season's growth begins.

   The nests of breeding birds are protected by law and it is an offence to knowingly destroy one that is being used or built. It is good practice to check a hedge for nests before cutting. If you find a nest, then you can simply delay cutting for the short period that the birds will be using the nest.

Traffic – Motor traffic lies behind a significant proportion of the bird mortality in many suburban and urban areas. If your garden is situated next to a road then it is worth considering how the layout of the garden can be modified to reduce the chances of a bird colliding with a motor vehicle. Positioning a new mixed-species hedgerow next to the road may, in time, attract birds to nest in the hedge, putting them at increased risk of collision. Similarly, the positioning of nestboxes and feeding stations should be given due consideration.

These different risks might make it appear that gardens are not a particularly safe place for birds, raising the question of "should you be trying to attract birds to them in the first place?" However, it is essential to realise that there are also risks associated with living in woodland, farmland or any other habitat. Some of the risks are the same (*e.g.* predation – though by different predators), some are not. Gardens (if managed sensibly) are no more risky than other habitats.

Pied Wagtail – Jill Pakenham

Books

The following publications include some of the best books available on wildlife gardening, providing additional detail to some of the topics covered here.

Rejuvenating a Garden, by Stephen Anderton (1998). Kyle Cathie Ltd., London. ISBN 1-85626-276-6.

A Handbook of Native Trees and Shrubs, by Charlotte de la Bedoyere (2004). New Holland Publishers Ltd. ISBN 1-84330-606-9.

Hostas, by Sandra Bond (1992), Ward Lock Ltd, London. ISBN 0-7063-7060-0. This book was republished as part of a volume entitled *The Complete Guide to Foliage Planting* (1997). ISBN 0-7063-7581-5. Also by Ward Lock Ltd, London.

Garden Natural History, by Stefan Buczacki (2007). Collins New Naturalist, Harper Collins, London, ISBN 0-00-713993-4.

Foodplant List for the Caterpillars of Britain's Butterflies and Larger Moths, by Tim Crafer (2005). Atropos. 124 pages. ISBN 0-9551-0860-8.

The BTO Nestbox Guide, by Chris du Feu (2003). British Trust for Ornithology, Thetford. ISBN 1-902576-81-0.

English Plants for Your Garden, by Jill, Duchess of Hamilton, Penny Hart & John Simmons (2000). Frances Lincoln Publishers. ISBN 0-7112-1435-2.

Native Trees and Shrubs for Your Garden, by Jill, Duchess of Hamilton & Christopher Humphries (2005). Frances Lincoln Publishers. ISBN 0-7112-2215-0.

The Birdwatcher's Garden, by Hazel & Pamela Johnson (1999), Guild of Master Craftsman Publications Ltd, Lewes. ISBN 1-86108-135-9.

Plants for All Seasons, by Andrew Lawson (1999). Frances Lincoln Publishers. ISBN 0-71121-392-5.

Wildlife Gardening, by Charlie Ryrie (2003). Cassell Illustrated, London. ISBN 1-84403-035-0.

Birds and Berries, by Barbara and David Snow (1988), T & A D Poyser, Calton. ISBN 0-85661-049-6.

Meadows and Cornfields, by Jenny Steel (2001). Webbs Barn Designs, Kingston Bagpuize. ISBN 0-95411-160-5.

Wildlife Ponds, by Jenny Steel (2002). Webbs Barn Designs, Kingston Bagpuize. ISBN 0-95411-161-3.

Butterfly Gardening, by Jenny Steel (2004). Webbs Barn Designs, Kingston Bagpuize. ISBN 0-95411-162-1.

No Nettles Required: The reassuring truth about wildlife gardening, by Ken Thompson (2006). Eden Project Books, Transworld Publishers. ISBN 1-90391-968-1.

Wildlife Gardening for Everyone, by Malcolm Tate (2006), RHS & The Wildlife Trusts, Think Publishing, London. ISBN 1-84525-016-8.

The BTO/CJ Garden BirdWatch Book, by Mike Toms (2006), British Trust for Ornithology, Thetford. ISBN 1-902576-73-X.

RHS Pruning and Training, 2nd revised ed., by Christopher Brickell & David Joyce (2003) Dorling Kindersley, London. ISBN 1-40530-073-6.

References

Alexander, K., Butler, J. & Green, T. (2006). The number of species of insect associated with various trees. *British Wildlife* **18**: 18–28.

Bhatti, M. & Church, A. (2001). Cultivating natures; homes and gardens in late modernity. *Sociology* **35**: 365–383.

Cannon, A. (1999). The significance of private gardens for bird conservation. *Bird Conservation International* **9**: 287–297.

Chamberlain, D.E., Cannon, A.R. & Toms, M.P. (2004). Associations of garden birds with gradients in garden habitat and local habitat. *Ecography* **27**: 589–600.

Churcher, P.B. & Lawton, J.H. (1987). Predation by domestic cats in an English village. *Journal of Zoology, London,* **212**: 439-455.

Crafer, T. (2005). Foodplant List for the Caterpillars of Britain's Butterflies and Larger Moths. Atropos. 124 pages ISBN 0-9551-0860-8.

Newson, S.E., Woodburn, R.J.W., Noble, D.G., Baillie, S.R. & Gregory, R.D. (2005). Evaluating the Breeding Bird Survey for producing national population size and density estimates. *Bird Study* **52**: 42–54.

Southwood, T.R.E. (1961). The number of species of insect associated with various trees. *Journal of Animal Ecology* **30**: 1–8.

Toms, M.P. (2007). Are gardens good for birds or birdwatchers? *British Wildlife* **19**: 77–83.

Suppliers

The following organisations and companies are stockists and suppliers of plants and wildlife-gardening materials.

British Wildflower Plants Burlingham Gardens, 31 Main Road, North Burlingham, Norfolk, NR13 4TA. 01602-716615. www.wildflowers.co.uk

CJ WildBird Foods Ltd The Rea, Upton Magna, Shrewsbury, Shropshire, SY4 4UR. 0800-731-2820. www.birdfood.co.uk

Emorsgate Seeds Limes Farm, Tilney All Saints, King's Lynn, Norfolk, PE34 4RT. 01553-829028. www.wildseed.co.uk

Flora Locale Denford Manor, Hungerford, Berkshire, RG17 0UN. 01488-680457 www.floralocale.org

Flower Farms Carvers Hill Farm, Shalborne, Marlborough, Wiltshire, SN8 3PS. www.wildflowerfarms.com

Landlife Wildflowers National Wildflower Centre, Court Hey Park, Liverpool, L16 3NA. 0151-737-1819. www.wildflower.org.uk

Natural Gardens Greenacre, Fakenham Road, Great Ryburgh, Norfolk, NR21 7AG. 01328-829309. www.naturalgardens.co.uk

The Natural Gardener The Steppes, Hope under Dinmore, Nr Leominster, Herefordshire, HR6 0PP. 01568-611729. www.thenaturalgardener.co.uk Online supplier of organic, biodegradable and sustaining gardening products.

Wiggly Wigglers Lower Blakemere Farm, Blakemere, Herefordshire, HR2 9PX. 01981-500391. www.wigglywigglers.co.uk. Suppliers of wormeries, garden composters and wildflower seeds and plants.

Organisations

The following organisations can provide very useful advice on wildlife gardening and those species associated with gardens.

Bat Conservation Trust Unit 2 15 Cloisters House, 8 Battersea Park Road, London, SW8 4BG. 020-7627-2629. www.bats.org.uk

British Trust for Ornithology The Nunnery, Thetford, Norfolk, IP24 2PU. 01842-750050. www.bto.org

BTO/CJ Garden BirdWatch. 16,000 participants, a year-round study providing valuable information on how birds use gardens and how this use changes throughout the year and over the longer-term. A free enquiry pack is available from GBW, Room G4, BTO, The Nunnery, Thetford, Norfolk, IP24 2PU. 01842-750050. www.bto.org/gbw

British Wildflower Plants Burlingham Gardens, 31 Main Road, North Burlingham, Norfolk, NR13 4TA. 01602-716615. www.wildflowers.co.uk

Bumblebee Conservation Trust School of Biological & Environmental Sciences, University of Stirling, Stirling, FK9 4LA. 01786-467818. www.bumblebeeconservationtrust.co.uk

Butterfly Conservation Manor Yard, East Lulworth, Dorset, BH20 5QP. 0870-774-4309. www.butterfly-conservation.org

Cottage Garden Society c/o Clive Lane, Brandon, Ravenshall, Betley, Cheshire, CW3 9BH. www.thecgs.org.uk

Garden Organic (HDRA) Garden Organic Ryton, Coventry, Warwickshire, CV8 3LG. 0247-630-3517 www.gardenorganic.org.uk

Herpetological Conservation Trust 665A Christchurch Road, Boscombe, Bournemouth, Dorset, BH1 4AP. 01202-391319. www.herpconstrust.org.uk

Mammal Society 3 The Carrnades, New Road, Southampton, SO14 0AA. 0238-023-7874 www.abdn.ac.uk/mammal

Natural Gardens Greenacre, Fakenham Road, Great Ryburgh, Norfolk, NR21 7AG. 01328-829309. www.naturalgardens.co.uk

Plantlife International 14 Rollestone Street, Salisbury, Wiltshire, SP1 1DX. 01722-342730. www.plantlife.org.uk

Postcode Plants www.nhm.ac.uk/nature-online/life/plants-fungi/postcode-plants/

Royal Horticultural Society 80 Vincent Square, London, SW1P 2PE. 0845-260-5000. www.rhs.org.uk

UFAW The Old School, Brewhouse Hill, Wheathampstead, Hertfordshire, AL4 8AN. 01582-831818. www.ufaw.org.uk

Wildlife Gardening with Jenny Steel. Jenny has produced a series of books on wildlife gardening and tutors courses on the subject. More information can be found at www.wildlife-gardening.co.uk

Wildlife Trusts The Kiln, Waterside, Mather Road, Newark, Nottinghamshire, NG24 1WT. 01636-677711. www.wildlifetrusts.org